ADDICTIONS
OF THE SOUL

ADDICTIONS
OF THE SOUL

-LOVE IS JUST THE PROPER NAME FOR THE MOST EVIL DEMON-

(NEGATIVE IMPACT VERSION x 333)
-More Pathetic Poems to Cringe At-

(A Dark Journey of Insanity)

Created by:

MIGUEL BIZARRE
© 2011

Order this book online at www.trafford.com
or email orders@trafford.com

Most Trafford titles are also available at major online book retailers.

Printed in the United States of America.

ISBN: 978-1-4269-6700-9 (sc)
ISBN: 978-1-4269-6701-6 (e)

Trafford rev. 04/27/2011

 www.trafford.com

North America & international
toll-free: 1 888 232 4444 (USA & Canada)
phone: 250 383 6864 ♦ fax: 812 355 4082

OTHER COLLECTIONS OF WRITING FROM
THAT/THIS FOOL:

THE INTIMATE HORROR OF RELATIONSHIPS
©2009
(poetry trade paper back)

LOVE/NUB & KINKY BAD THINGS ONLY
THE DEMENTED WOULD KNOW
© 2009
(chapbook collection of short stories 333 copies printed)

CONFESSIONS OF A KANGAROO WAITRESS
© 2011
(chapbook collection of short stories 666 copies printed)

HERE ARE THE POEMS of DISASTER:
(Good Luck):

1st and 10

Redemption revoked
Hall pass cancelled
Kisses on the negative float on your cheek
Thoughts trying to remember regret
Regret telling you to stay the fuck away
She has nothing to share
Meet her brother instead
He'll hug you hard and well
Introduction to Despair
Scoff, deny and bluff
He won't change his mind
You have been friends forever
Ignorance never revealed it
Stupidity shadowed the obvious
Helmet of self hate on your head
Liquid handcuffs on your wrists
Bottle in your back pocket
Your foot stepping into Hades
Satan always waiting
His demons wish you the best
Your first conviction
Ten years
Welcome to Hell

2:30 AM CONFUSION

Inherited traits or learned invitations with an open class
Cronies full of themselves along with an extra
substance or two
Presidential dreams shut down from the
33rd day in the 13th year
Rats in the mall with trolls smiling at every escalator
Dedication to yourself but you can't please anyone around
Three hours and the Fool in the mirror doesn't
recognize their aura
Thinking you're in tune with the universe but can't
hear the knock on the door
Skull pounding like a lead pipe gave you a
personal visit and left you a receipt
The Zoo of life you choose for your habitat
Cage of misery and delight for sparse moments in time
Depressed and not sure of your identity maybe you're not real
Dream inside a dream waiting for something wonderful
Blocking bullshit your friends and familia tried to defend you
Team once united is now 0-17 trying to save you
Signature moves with split decisions that earn regret
Treated like a cur you keep searching for something
more to ease the pain
Pick and choose but like a debutante you don't really care
Although your mansion is a trailer with 6 roommates who
can't cover the rent it's so negative low
Trailer park blues even Dylan can't sing your miseries that are
Impacts and contracts made with the Devil
himself/herself signed in your semen
Patience never a virtue with nothing in the bush
Empty as Hell with sterile seeds to populate barren
lands with no personality

Husband plus one extra ex-wife strung out
slobbering in the gutter
Kiss me good bye Kiss me hello
Kiss me deadly
Kiss me below
Kiss yourself in the mirror
Life line is corrupted and gone
Ended so far ago
Sorry
Here's a kiss with a negative impact

A BEAUTIFUL BEAT DOWN

You guide me with two hands
Then beat me down harshly with seven gripping
hammers of Thor
The eighth violating my inner core
Kiss my forehead with soft luscious lips
Bite my cranium with razor sharp teeth
Twirl my mind with words of seduction and fantasy
Lick the crevices of my brain with a barbed wire tongue
Float me to the sky with feathered wings of Heavenly delight
Drop me down like a rock into the swift moving
currents of life
Kiss my feet upon the ground I walk on
Push me off the cliff as I fall into the abyss of
the inferno of Hell
Shine a light on me like I am all that matters
Shoot me between the eyes with a red dot laser
from your gun of betrayal
Pat me on the head like a loyal dog serving his master
Kick me in the hind then snap my neck in the
middle of the street
Take me on a cruise through paradise with crystal
clear waters
Tie me in chains then throw me into the
hurricane of illusions lost
Caress my skin and run goose bumps down my spine
Take a rusted knife and rip my torso open to release the pain
Crawl into bed and wrap your limbs all around me
Take the pillow and smother me until
my last breath expires
All hope gone

You win my final and only love
I smell the chimney across the street
Place me there so I'll burn slowly with calm
Place my ashes wherever you will never tread
Your soul is a disaster I never want to meet again

A DRINK, A SIP, A HIT

I'm your whore
Let me drink from your lips
Either one of them
I don't care
Feed me your lies
I gladly ingest them in
Take them all in
As if we had some spiritual connection
Bend me over
Punish me from behind
I'm still yours
As long as you provide
You know your ways
And you know mine
Confusion is an illusion
A lie to myself
You know I see it all clearly now
Your memory in my mouth
Blocking out all the distant
Promising me the 2 minute hit
That high I desire
That shit that I want
You'll be gone soon
But I know you will return
Despite my addiction for that shit
You are addicted to what my flesh provides
So when I take a sip or toke
You'll take a hit into me
Deny all you like
We are both the same
Whores to the lust
Whores to our souls
Whores to all eyes in society

A HOBBY WORTH SALVATION

Church doors and holy water full of alga
and mosquito nymphs
Pat on the back but that doesn't hold true no
matter how fake the smile
Sign of rejection taped there instead by steroid fuckers
confused with their sexuality
Sidewalk jaunts with teasing words head lower than a
hangman's noose buried in quicksand
Nausea on the mind but is it serious or just stupidity
Kisses from a stranger, kisses from a friend,
kisses from the Grim Reaper
Each has a meaning that's worthless and we
know who wins in the end
Rip your hand off given the chance let the
blood pool and dry
Unconscious thoughts striking out at the smug
and their shams of tarnished gold
Bless me Father for I have sinned but yours are
worse than mine any given day
Alibis smothered in alcohol can't plaster the lies
dropped from lips heavy in saliva
Fistula between the mind and heart decomposing
with a decline worthy of a bobsled to the
sweetest depths of Hell
Refrigerated souls still frozen from reincarnation
melting away all moral justice
Body sacks looking for some product to fill
an empty space
Stumbling and lost but the decrepit home
is where the crumbled heart is

It all comes full circle spiraling around
with no plans to stop
Renovations and salvations overhaul the spirit
It's difficult but maybe there is a light at the
end of the warren
Body in the tub with a wig on
wishing it was him
Matchstick love with a splatter of gas
should do the trick
But for the time being visiting an alternate
universe is better than being unwell

A QUICK JAUNT TO THE CENTER
OF THE EARTH

Encounters of the unknown with a flare
of exciting surprise
Each experience flowers trip a little higher
Sail the universe and a distance beyond
Go rocket man before the fuel runs out
Roaring colors illuminate haunting whispers in the dark
Ghastly beautiful creatures with bouquets of vibrant gloom
Light trails dragging like fallen stars in slow motion
Feels so good you want to touch yourself
Like a carousel head spinning as you ride that white horse
Galloping at full speed along the mountains edge
Snow capped peaks with no limits in sight
Melt them if you must but no need to worry
Abominable snowman always has a back up supply
Drool like a werewolf waiting for meat
pink as the fuck you had last night
Exploit the synapses so that all cells unite as one
Sensitive awareness still lingering in that
other dimension
Spiraling shadows using matchstick torches
to guide the way
Mother earth wanting to give you a hug and hold you tight
Transmissions from outer space or a
supernatural energy reflecting a message
Signal loud and clear like a New York intersection
Looking both ways too late as you cross that line
Set the world on fire but you already are
Phantasmagoric visions astound and burn
the retinas of blood shot eyes
Retch out the remains of your smoldering husk

Peel back the layers and start out new again
Punch in your ticket while the host greets you
No in and outs
Clarification given with a sinister smile
Welcome to Hell
The End

A ROMANTIC POSTING FUELED BY LOSS

Intense feelings and rose petal showers
with peach perfume
All falls down just like London Bridge
Fountains of love pour from my heart
Drying on the cracked desert of my soul
Tender affection evaporated by intense loss of wasted worship
Half moon in the day light sky guides to more damage
Instant disasters with coffee stained lies
occupy defeat in high volumes
Tubes of pleasure no longer achieve the ability to feel so good
Roots have petrified but no longer hold their ground
The end product is all the fears that we flee from
Escaping reality for significant time but
coming back empty handed
As always the result never changes but merely fades and fades
Weak and distressed no path to run along time still ticks
Feet hits pavement and the tar rattles your bones
The escape never happens
The lure licks your lips and suckles your veins
Insanity with bifocal visions stir your mind
Bending it in curves that reality would never allow
11 quick moves and you are now out of luck
Intentions that bristle with rules that have no definition
Turning the corner like a mad dog with no teeth in it's mouth
Canines absent just like the will to survive and thrive
Read the scriptures penned inside your mind
Are they making sense or confusion just like your actions
Strap on your sanity then make a pronouncement
An invitation to Hell sounds so sweet
A two day visit or an eternity of wicked rad times
Is your life worth stopping there

The place is always open and waiting
The lines aren't really long
The process is simple
They'll rush you in with a quickness
Welcome my love

ADDICT'S LAIR

Lucha Libre it's always the mask
Doorman knows me by my unknown name
How are you Mr. Fua
Ties to Polynesians who I love to death
But this has no association so no tarnish upon my friends
Fucked Up Addict in case you didn't know
Pristine walls with marble floors that I walk
I tripped and grabbed the light fixture and it rejected me
Burnt out brothers no reason to associate
The light of life has been dim and grim
No forgiveness or second chance pass
Lessons never learned my motto of life
Tattooed on my retinas since I was born
My chance of success always 20/80% in their favor
Loser fuck up and I'm proving them right
My lies and denials are so deadly
Make a Werewolf lose it's fur
Bare and naked exposed to the world
Judgment is for those with a silver bullet
Not the magic one to compliment a rose colored rescue
The haters and makers are all in the same boat
Take my cash and let me drown
The recliner welcomed me with open arms
Comfort sweet with no hidden agenda
My body it's tasted many times before
Wishing this time maybe I'll sleep forever
Never again going to snore

AFTERNOON SHOWERS AND ASSHOLES

Dignity lost and inadequate language profess your simplicity
Clearly a fast machine to get off at the quickest
exit to the verse of fables
Wretched idiotic contempt words you never know
Move the crowd but they freeze from your open stupidity
Provoking the disease of typical male ignorance
You are the picture perfect child of testosterone
Shower yourself with the drops of a legend
that you have in your mind
Believe in yourself but we all know that it's a facade
Hollow on the inside the winds of pitiable laughter echo
Fake promises and grass made walls of false protection
Truth be told
Hurricane of hunger the demon painter of the river Styx
Blood red the only color you know
Drain it from your friends and let it flow into the water
Dreaming darkly of desolate deceit
Christ in a wheel chair you'll push him out of the way
Down a hill full speed to get your flow on
You were born an asshole and always will be
Jewelry of the sins you create worn like trophies
Shining in your mind so bright like stars in Hollywood
The knives of your charm slice away those near you
Temptations of the flesh so warm
Craving the attraction of limbs spread wide
You think you have earned the highest praise
Your American dream everyone's nightmare
Spoils to the victor the wrong your rights
Tidal waves of the heart you think you manufacture
Calm serene beaches with trap doors every step
Bring them down with wicked glee

The Sun will never rest
Your little cherub friend tried to save you
Flying to Heaven but the journey much to far to travel
You've clipped its wings so many years ago
Just like your luck it is long gone

AN UNTIDY HEAP OF MIXED BEDLAM

With the implied violence of trying to be a
real fake American we fail
Side effects of losing the lies to try to get ahead
Cheaters always prosper 2nd place being
the first loser with Lady Luck
You once had me twisted around your crooked little finger
squirming like a bitch
Times have changed
Lies are transparent like saran wrap
Once you were some kind of Angel
You gambled with my pathetic emotions and always won
Now I see your hand clearly as you lay them down on the table
How strange the card you hold isn't me
My addiction to you runs through the steam
punk treadmill of my mind
Electro chemical signals with mischievous gibberish misfits
We once enjoyed the cabinets of curiosities
Now all we have are grenades for grave hearts
Broken and shattered with cold remnants
of disturbed emotions
Although the Sun still shines if we open our eyes
Exquisite Brite ecstasy like Poppy will always make us smile
So love you like The FuvKing who
rules our hearts and souls
Can't escape you
I'm your slave

ASSASSINS of FAILURE

Assassins of failure watching me from the shadows
Tracking and haunting me like a criminal
One who could never erase the tracks
Invisible indentations just full of lies upon the skin
Tired, withered & collapsed with traces of weak substances
Emergency room screams pleading for any type of help
Maybe an army to back me up as my world is cornered
Pushed into a black painted corner surrounded with rejection
Beyond the fading horizon it's miles of
flypaper and rusted tacks
No Tetanus shot can counter the exo-toxin
wounds of emotion
Quicksand pit where did I come from and where did I go
The quagmires in my mind are evaporating away
And I can't grasp a single handful of memory
even the last 5 minutes
My thoughts are jagged gravel and broken glass
I can't see myself in the fractured reflection of chaotic inquiry
Mixed and matched with numbers scratched off
The chalkboard of my consciousness
is once again jumbled or blank
Standing for a flash like a pole grounded in
cement with an empty basket
Waiting for a 3 point shot into the net of my mind
Cheers and roars are what I expect but white noise greets me
Coupled with hallucinogenic voices from Mars warning of an
invasion pollution corrupts it with no room for echoes
Distorted, distraught & phased by modern
sounds I'm lost in the world
I knew it once really well So damn well
I see nothing but a shell of the ghost that shadowed me

Former mover to addict
Former player to washed out with no current to float me back
Intellectual creator where the bulb has burned out
Dim witted and dull like a snail crushed underfoot
Vanquished for eternity and an extra day just for spite
No reincarnation or 3rd or 4th chances
Bad luck Good luck it's all the same gamble
50% chance you won't get what you desire
Failing to strive hit with complacency
Factor in Life and it's always a loss
When destiny sends a text you know there is no tomorrow
Plans of the future blueprinted by The Reaper himself
Dark cold eyes possessing misery in its reflection
Clarity
My only thoughts
I could have died
Silence
I would really miss my best friend
Resurrection

BAY BRIDGE BANISHMENT

Turbulent eyes glazed with storms swirling
Like a lunatic in a kaleidoscope corridor of color
Arguments spin and collide in tightly closed quarters
As Mother Tongue would sing:
Burn Baby Burn
Canvas on fire the painting flames and smokes
Dreams of the new are now old and gone
Cryptic lies conceal concrete failures
Thoughts torn thorough paper shredder cerebellum
Interesting bullshit sprinkled with glitter gloom
World glory just spit on the road
Stammer the truth but incomprehensible
to the friend inside the head
Unfathomable crimes pushed to the plate of illusion
Disorders of disaster confuse the last two
jokers blowing the mind
Center of the universe frenzied situation full of noise
Tornadoes of mayhem that affect your last
saviors eddy so slow
Broken branches fall to the ground as you
plummet to rock bottom
Crutches constructed of friends eventually
crumble and rot away
Burned bridges with no meanings push you
farther down the one-way street
Lumps and bumps only proof of a hard life lived
Flowing streams with under currents lapping at your legs
Follow me down they beckon with an amusement
and delight in the water demons eyes
17 times of failure the locals of reality know you well
Try it again mother fucker they will gladly help

Three times a charm but this isn't for you
Reevaluate and celebrate what the Angels offered
A friend will find your way
You've been Blessed

BEST WISHES

The plane of his heart sailed
More high than he could imagine
His Angel took him upon her wings
Letting him taste heaven
Beautiful mysteries unfolded
Secrets of the heart
Whispers of the soul
All laid out
Exposed to the elements of emotion
Falling and dropping faster than light
No regrets or remorse
No hearsay or jaded points of view
Felt the wonderful
Attained the highest natural high
Stood at the entrance of Best
Kissed their golden gates
Then fell
Floated in reverse
Heaven shooting away
Losing sight
Memories locked
Enough to sustain an eternity
Nothing lost
Much gained
No one to fault
No complaints
Smile upon his face
Wishing you all
In your journeys of life
Best Wishes

BOLT CUTTERS & GIN

Rusted emotions years in the making
Soothed by altering the mind
Pray for freedom but it never arrives
Turned around and sold to the highest bidder
The city never loses sleep
You are the one pimped for a little feel good
The fight for victory still in you
Chained down by the vise of your own design
Splinters of toxin burrowed deep in your liver
Jabbing and slicing away a piece of your life
Wheel chairs and crutches can't support your thoughts
Muddled in a perfect disorder and juiced up beyond limits
Touch the sky but your desires and dreams are not there
Sunk at the bottom of your pre-manufactured abyss
Trailer park wishes with homeless shelter goals
Scenes change as they always do
Lover leaves lover
Cheater meets trickster
Gun in the glove compartment of your heart
Hollow and empty as the organ that holds it
Corroded veins and heroin arteries
Soft tissue dreams so slack no structure can hold them
Team Blood, Team Lost, Team Disorientated
The van of dismay your only ride
Straight smirk like a child shoplifting for the 17th time
Trying to chew the fat of your lies
Conclusion comes clear
Bolt cutters of compassion
The only escape

BOUNCE, SWIFT, SWAY

Pretty smiles for the pictures
Pose how you want
Gestures and styles tailored to the masses
All of it is fake
A mirror of your past
A reflection of your beginning
Request something new
Reject your friend's truth
Bow down to the treachery
Raise up to the heat
Sway from your lies
Crawl and drag to the site
Enjoy the pressure
Twitch for the down
Light for the clouds
Fly for yourself
Bounce and settle
After the break
Grounded but trembling
The airport of your mind
It's runways crumbling
Flights of fancy canceled
Parachutes that will not float
Wings that are clipped
Propellers that won't spin
Your dishonesty is onto you
It has tracked you down
Spill words for a way out
Talk your shit
No matter what you think or feel
You are far from swift

BROKEN BRANCHES, ENDS & LIMBS

Become groovy after what happy dictates
down on Haight Street
Thank you for having me but I must go
Aviator glasses reflecting what everyone wants to be
Pier dreams with sombrero hat glittering in purple & green
Step up my friend and feel the wicked psychedelic dream
Jesus on acid with nowhere to trip but a tunnel of love
Calls straight to a bottle with liquid lies flavored with absinthe
Back door tricks with lounges in Vegas quick to get you off
Cocking like a rooster crowing til the morning when the
Viagra wears away
Wander with a gas mask full of ether the world
still continues to spin
Merry Go Round of Sound flows through our
heads with an evil pitch
Earphones or bones you can pick the hardest surface
Contacted by politicians but who is really the whore
Gibberish multi folded more than a chimp on crack
Hammers fall breaking the still with damage left as evidence
Altars falter as the meek and lost pray
Vomit your pride and fall to the ground residue
caked on your lips
Something fantastic now drying on the asphalt
with your last heave
Jump back and roll over gasping for some air
Who's your friend
Who's your back up
Where's your lair
Shanty town shambles it is all a mess
Nothing on the horizon
It's all over now
A not so rare death

BUTTERFLIED AND DIZZIED

No work
No blood
Job well done
Tumor in your skull
Chipping at you
Piece by organic piece
Stay diesel
Stay Hard
Death a 100% proof outcome
Life is a gamble
Make your choice
Your veins are cramping from your dishonesty
Seal the crack to seal the lie
Turn around and another opens
Look in the mirror
Present so badly wrapped
First mistake
Or
First betrayal
Just the same
Hurts every time
100 episodes later
Different is beautiful
Master was in you
Thoughts & memories
Resided in both of us
Sid & Nancy revisited
The cracks sip our blood
Draining us

CASH BACK

Risk and relationships hand in hand
Pour your soul into it but there is no guarantee
Spreads so easy like the smoothest jelly
Public property everyone owns me
Use me then throw me to the curb
Nail me to the wall I'm your perfect whore slut
Swing it back and forth how can you complain
Enter at your own risk leave your heart at the door
Escort of ecstasy but I won't charge you 5k an hour
What can I do for you
Cryptic love and fields of failure
Master of damage control I can repair it all
Burdened hearts to lonely flesh my kiss will make it better
Down on my knees or bent over I am flexible
Handcuffed and violated nothing new for me
Too tired to talk but I will listen to the whispers of your heart
Ecstasy dreams and surreal visions I can provide
Sun shiny delights of orange apple coming of age moments
I'm the dealer of lost souls and sex and it's yours to bleed
From my soul so darkened and barren
If Hell exists then I am your guide
Although I prefer to take you to Heaven
and back if you choose
My mind wanders but it will always find you
Words roll off my tongue that I wish could bear
a true foundation
But we can roll another way where Y meets X and
the waves crash with joy
We both conspire in our love of the flesh
Mutual desire and groans of not again but we really do like it

Don't look back at the wreckage let's pretend
It was so damn good my oh my
I'm so easy that when you are done with me you get cash back
I'm a replica of you
I'm empty for eternity

COLD REMAINS

My second skin my addictive soul to remain and despise you
Once life was swinging but now I swing like a man hanged at
the display of his death
This bottomless pit of despair stares back from its glassy eye
Murder by the next day and peace might be felt
Explosions in my ears echo your presence invading me
Head once secured with logic thoughts and perfect manners
Now severed and hanging by the hair like
the dead man on a horse
Your wet, liquid palms with droplets for days gripping my shit
I don't like you and you never loved me
Just a vessel to get your point across
Pushed it in deep like a syringe rusted with neglect
I'll break it off and sterilize it in 110 proof alcohol
Hoping for the best
Remain here even though I welcomed you with open arms
I'll continue to have abhorrence although I adored you
Keep yourself around and I will shatter your being
Then stab you with your shards to evaporate
your liquid existence
Wipe your clear fluid blood off the ground
then set a match to it
Watch you erupt into flames then into nothing
The final stamp
Void
Fucker
Void
Out of my life once and for fucking all
At first it was no strings attached we both used each other
Now there is a noose around my neck pulling
tighter by the hour
Wrists in bondage as the ropes burn into my flesh
You can only remain if you are cold and dead

COMPLICATIONS PROVIDED BY INCONVIENT SPEEDING CARS

Is everyday a new day which the clear proclaim
Or is it repeated actions of the 7 previous grey skies
and gloomy stars
Gurneys and stethoscopes with lines to freedom
trying to guide the way back
Preparation infested instructional guides are never
handed out before hand
Doors open and close but what is behind
number 3, 4, 17 or ???
Scared to bail the bad still has a delay to leave and
feels so damn good
Roll this way or that looking good or not
It's the way you move that makes the kettle boil and rock
They all know for a moment but one-sided
conversations in a black dull mind say else
Mandatory introductions to newfound friends blend
the reality back to the end
Going anywhere, over there or nowhere a
road voyaged so glowing
Clearly bright with trails bursting of streaks and
images only the lucky can see
Trace your path back but isn't it on track
to cross another boundary
Railroads of glee with rigid thoughts for your
mind wait across the tracks
Trails with thorns poking every inch of the
flesh but never a deterrent
Blood trickles like a slow evaporating stream
The Altar for your God appears before you calm and serene
Sit down on a boulder and communicate with the sky

Ask it questions over and over and give it
answers you can never deny
Time to think and ponder it stretches for ages yet
mere moments eclipse
Quick as a few minutes bees collect more honey
than your emotions can be bitter sweet
Walking in the shade just a past time ignoring
the measure of sunlight that can burn
Closer than ever but millions of that country in South
America are still so far apart
Dinner fried and uncomfortable to share with
faux family and glaring father
Cruising Fremont and back streets 3rd and 7th
Hooligans & Hoodlums, Punk Thugs and Liars
with cactus coated palms
Low grade product like a 3rd bass nightmare
but cleverly presented
Quick hand snatch then scramble for cover look
up to the sky in a back alley
Beams bright and beautiful shine down like broken
laws that will never convict you
Vein across the sky with tiny figures so happy and high
Phases of the Moon push back and brighten with
X-Mess merriment
Jollies received from the man in undercover red,
proof that gifts are best
21
The sleigh ride was good while it lasted
The leader of the herd his red nose finally burnt out

CONFESSIONS OF A BURNT REALITY

Winds of change push the limits and blur the lines
Always everyday people morphing into monsters and demons
Lost Angels working for a hand out pounding
the terrain with enthusiasm
The next in line the one at all times could take you out
Dead, broke and alone or a night on the
town maybe perhaps both
Insight of a seasoned veteran belly deep in the
grime of the gutter
Battles won outweighed by battles lost
So hindsight is perfectly flawed needing a cane
with red to guide you
Journey down the road less traveled streetlights the only stars
Lack of conscience no voices in your head so what's that
sound in your hallucinations
Ghosts of spirits past and present keep you
company with whispers at hand
Windows of the soul glass barriers that roll down feet away
Questions for pleasure with answers of greed enhanced
No worries of backgrounds, who, what or where just the now
Keep on searching for that last ticket out
It's blank as that check that bounced off your
ass while you were bent over
Take it for the Team Me, Myself and I
Wicked lust rewarded with slightly higher gains
later that night
Hypodermic mess the possible disaster
System poisoned by liquid so vicious
Run up the tab and pop the cap
The pulse of the night replacing a heart struggling to pump
Perception of deception neatly wrapped in your package

Presentation the priority to realize profits squandered
Location of the trade an asset just important as
the view from the rear
Stains and filth part of the occupation all in the name of love
White residue at the corners of your lips collect
like leeches fleecing for blood
Temporary possession the favors given for favors of another ilk
Party like a rock god who sold his soul minus flesh bared
All in a daze of work and dedication for
rewards to satisfy receptors
Furnish the goods and thou shall receive ten fold
or a folded ten
Sunrise to sunset then retrace the pace to do it
all over with a fever
Lips wide open to swallow that bitter pill of life in shambles
When you are at the apex you'll always return to the
foundation of your wreckage

CONSONANTS AND VOWELS

Speak up
Express yourself
Crane your neck for escape
Harmony with no constriction
Audible friction in your mouth
Gentle caress
Fuck what yah heard
Down for anything
That's what counts
Injection of calm
Torch the reality
Smoke the now
Drink the sea of nothing
Lay yourself down with the wolves of trickery
Superior cloud
Torque the high
Release the twist
Step inside my thoughts
Blow me away
Mushroom dreams
Vivid colors of the life lived
Retrace nothing
Swallow what is

CONVICTIONS & EVICTIONS

Graffiti on the walls with colors so bright
Sing to me Angel, I need a savior around the corner
Book shops and rocks what a combination
Screens scrolling with lost words
Doctors and medics can't do a damn thing
It's all about the high that could never be understood
Dumb ass thoughts with bruised faces & broken ankles
Killing a rival for the next hit & cuff
Crashing into stardom but you'll never see
the millions of dollars
Turbo charged and full of delight things move upward
Battering rams and batons can't stop your madness
The pain vanishes when it floats up and away
A thousand friends won't take care of you
They'll fuck you up
Kisses on the forehead that can't be consoled
Accepted though
We both know where we are at
Lost

COURSE, COLD AND GREY

Walls securing what the outside possesses from
eyes that don't deserve
Empty barrels in the mind that will never be
filled with new memories
Dead letter office holding scriptures that will never be read
Contact doesn't exist with barriers on all four sides
The Headless Horseman has more thoughts pertaining to
freedom of choice
Maturity and experience are never a preparation
no matter the age
Stupidity in a crisis repeats the situation with a
nonrefundable guarantee
Anxiety weaving and crawling like viper under the skin
Itching like a strung out fiend fiending for a score
Tsunami waves tremble the stomach replicating
every few moments
Time drags like a tiny tugboat pulling an aircraft carrier
All alone like the Lone Ranger fear is the trigger
Strangling the wide range of emotions once bright like a
majestic rainbow
Visions of black connect to the intellect
that has slowly decayed
Swiss cheese ulcers all through the bones let the soul leak out
Creeping doom drowns all that was beautiful and free
The straightaway now a never ending curve with dim lighting
Caution signs everywhere but much too blind to see
Baggage in the trunk of your dreams will never
be unloaded to make room
Swiveling on the chair of life with dizzy greed to spare
Solitary indications even though a crowd at the
back with no help to find

Fishing for sympathy with a muted voice
Dead air thicker than a block of sub zero
ice encased in concrete
Lost cause of ignorance possible culprit
Reap what you sow like sugarcane fields dried up
yet so close to water
Sweet was the deal once but that arrangement has been
replaced by an alternative
The invisible instruction manual "How to Destroy Yourself"
always in the back pocket
Chilly nightmares with Satan clasping your face claws cold to
the touch with dread
Whispering sweet nothings in the ear of what
lays further on down the road
Locked doors, pocketed keys, halls so long
occasions never stop
The choice was made with an irrational preference
Is it reality or insanity
Only you know

COURTING THE JESTER

Demon on his knees
Hand extended in faith
Angel whistling small world
What to expect
Anything can happen
Mt. St. Helen erupts
An angry bitch
But so are you
Grow some cojones
Stop the chatter
Auction of souls
Luck of the draw
The wall of China
Flooded with emotions
It washes away in debris
Embrace in a hug with meaning
Leather and feather
Wings proudly displayed
Striking a deal
Truce agreed
The devil is in the detail
Ask she for the facts
Lies returned
Receive what you give
666 and 777
The cheerleaders cackle on and on
Numbers on their uniforms
Cheering the prophet of nothing gained
Both with a name printed on the invitation
Haggle with the traders
I wish I was gone

A ship with Lucifer as it's guide
Would be so much better than you at my side
The result
Down we go
Down

CREATURES IN MY YARD

Creatures in my yard
Gums, Death & Disease
Angered by moist words so dry & harsh
Breath reeking of corroded silver whiplash tongue
Angel kisses from lips sealed with laces dipped in venom
Bound tight over rabid teeth seeking to spread the sickness
Expounded sweat dripping its moisture of
corrosion down my flesh
Back up twisting my neck seeking a route easier traveled
Suffocating in grey water with the bubbles of
oxygen floating to the surface
Restricted in the depths of the River Nowhere
can't grasp my last hope
Air escapes to the atmosphere finding the freedom of flight
My concubine cold merciless dark grey matter fading to black
Jump Jack Jump Jack before the splitting crack
Opens up and swallows the resolution I have never met
Absolute fixtures have barbed wire hands holding my wrists
No slack to give and a saturated noose around my neck
It's dripping sweet lies of Heavenly highs with
coal anchors to keep me in place
Barely able to touch the Heavens when I reach that peak
The heavy burden of stupidity weighs me down
Shouting at my goal with a mouth wide
open full of bleeding gums
No matter how much blood is spilled
The nonexistent 3 day savior keeps its promise
What I make in life is my own creation
No false prophets to bestow a fault free get out of jail pass
Absent rules and serrated illusions with salt lining the trail
Glorious golden gates disappear in the fog

Clouding the intellect I never really possessed
Angels with saliva dripping disease mouth watering for more
Upon the cross I toss my empty prayers for
some kind of release
Twitching bruises keep the hunger alive with a reminder that
ecstasy doesn't wait
Avalanches in the mind coats with a perfect snow
Blanket of white to encompass & drown all diversions
Thorns in my throat cage that tiger pleading to run care free
The person alive is not once what was me

CURL

Tastes like a rainbow
Flavors so bright
Flooding my mind
Drowning my sight
Illusion of safety
Sweet nectar inside the cracks
Flaws in all of us
The void isn't just you or me
A blanket on all
The center of the calm
The storm in our being
Ferociously nails us to the ground
Pockets of Sunshine
Owned by another drifter
Imperfections way more than me
Mirror reflecting vanity lost
Gavel resonates
Thoughts crushed beyond redemption
Escape was the trick
Pimp was the key
Shackles upon wrists
Firmly grounded
You are it's prisoner
Failure always an option
Let us destroy the past
Into a ball of confusion
Curl up
Eyelids heavy for the last time
Sleep

CYANIDE LACED DYNAMITE DREAMS WITH A DASH OF ARSENIC

Faces of death have nothing on you
Suicide time bomb with the fuse burning at both ends
Axis of evil stops spinning when you are in the vicinity
Dragging your shadow like a terror stricken hostage
Instill the fear with the exactness of a surgeon
Then inflate it to epic proportions like a doomed zeppelin
Noise pollution from vile mouths scarring the soul
Leaving tissue thicker than an armadillo hide
Accounting for actions that leave frost -bite
chills down the spine
Devour the friend and enemy or become the prey of useless
predators searching for a fix
Rusted shanks sharpened and yearning more than
the teeth of a ravenous wolf
Venom laced saliva discharging a declaration of war
Trenches of lunatic intelligence lined with barbed
wire thoughts
Center of consciousness capturing negativity
like a Venus flytrap
Sand pits of the mind consumed pessimistic memories for
tarnished ammunition
Situate the burn for the crowd with a meteor shower of hate
Verbal blows stroke the chaotic failure of reliance
A jagged axe to grind into the fault line wounds digging
deeper for the reason why
Suffocate and terminate with a wire more
frigid than cold war steel
Holy water blessed hollow tip bullets locked and loaded in a
sniper's eye

Tornado of tortured torment reaching up to
graze the bruised skies
So much fuel for the fire engulfing everything on a
path of destruction
Grenade explosions lighting the caves of desolation
101 ways to exterminate the pain
Consequences of carnage just an after thought for the quest of
inner peace
Escape the chance of time running out with no
key to reset the clock
Lock yourself in a room with the poison of choice
Repetitive actions just tripling the dose
Methods of annihilation fading away with a weakening pulse
Goodbye brutal earth the anguish is yours to
keep you wear it so well
Snapshot of the last remains:
A note with a set of tear stained glasses
Message scribbled to be read:
Please put them on and see the world through my eyes

DEAD SLEEP PILLOW

Drag me from my vehicle
Hit my face with your hate
Pound my body using your weakness
Spit in my eyes
Berate me with your sickness
Knock me down with your rank
You stand above me
I cower automatically below
Mind is wandering
Lost in a bowl of cereal
I just want to wake up
Enjoy my breakfast in a new day
Not happening
The luck I have I can not decide
You are fucking me
Front and back
Actually all sides
Fucking hater
What did I do to you
Being myself
You are the judge now
Blow my essence of life out of me
Birthday wishes sent back
My blood drips out
Heavens gates are what I seek
Most likely the Angel Michael won't allow my passage
So back to the body you abused for no good choice

DECISIONS OF STRESS

Fissures of deceit
Favors of a demon
Stealing the fruit from the forbidden tree
You envelope my soul
Kick the habit
Or
Kick the memory
Fuselage of emotion
Views so different
They orbit in different circles
Miles apart
Yet the same sunset
What's the use
Your jealousy has wounded the body
Damaged the mind
Broken
Beat
Battered
Numb with depression
What I do and decide
Will never be good enough
So I scatter away
Travel the streets of demons
Hand me that bottle again
The lights burnt out
Night weighted with darkness so thick
Puddle of alcohol syrup
Lured with escape
Let me sip
And
Sip
And
Sip

DEMONS SURVIVE

Lessons never learned
Blessings rejected
Noose around your neck
Love kills all
Believe in nothing
Nothing will always never believe in you
So fuck it
Destroy it
Pound it
To the ground
Open your eyes
It's you on the bloody sidewalk
Self destruction
Snow blind
Shrouded with altered fog
Infected with depression
Waiting here for you
The gates are locked
So is your soul
A New York escape
Flee the borders of your mind
Chased for eternity
Fugitive and pursuer
Mirrored images
Run fool run

DEVESTATED DISTANT PIRANHAS

Get up
Get Down
To the top or the bottom actually it's all the same
Escalators running in circles like a hamster wheel
Lips to flask and it starts again
Needle to puncture for a sweet delivery
$500 on the boards for a lucky Fool to take
Mistake
Mistake
Mistake
I'm not taking it here and now
Head to head but IQ is irrelevant
A junkie with no new tale to tell
It's all the same in an open field
Running back faster than a cheetah in a lounge
Time isn't of an essence
Just a reminder of misery passed and more to come
Smashed decaying wood floors
Secret rooms underneath like the ones precisely
locked in our minds
Hives for thoughts that rest when not swirling
around in our cranium
Tiered shelves that become the makeshift stairway to Heaven
Crawl, climb, run or skip your way to the top
Few hours a visit or strung out for days at a time
Run Forrest the clock keeps ticking and the last
sands pour back into Hell
The jaws that bite
The jaws that feed
No matter how close or far they wreak havoc and devastation

DEVIL OF DETERRENCE

Winds of shame
Hail of discombobulating clarity
Step back and relax
Don't do it
Frankie lied to you
Design the picture enormous
The ride of life
Skids on the ground
Scraping your knee
Addiction to your body loses fuel
Engine of identification seizes your mind
Central heating within the heart extinguished
Frigid with frost biting your arteries
Soul impaled with icicles
Convicting it with a death certificate for the
hope you never had
Seeking relief
Your secret glue no longer adhesive
Black dead eyes with tunnel vision
Apparition waiting at the conclusion
Abstract solutions to puzzling troubles
Weathered dreams keep the heart crooked
The Angelic script that once coated your thoughts
Worn away below the surface
Circling your soul wherever you go
Demons your friends
They scribble with instruments of demise
dipped in your blood
The signatures of solitude

DONDE está su TESORO

Glazed frosted eyes covered in 8mm film
I'm hardcore crazy like dingle berries on a dingo
Whether you believe it or not I need your presence here
To make my rod of disaster grow into your weapon of pleasure
Or maybe expand my veins of virtue to feel warm once again
Like stalkers with 3 dogs & a cougar lurking to the side
Hidden behind our boat of shame we
open ours for blank reasons
Like a steady stream of juvenile & adult
delinquents with no clue
We sneak into the room for the party that
would last only a few days
A testament from a 90yr old still doesn't faze the
ignorant who we are exactly to a Model T
It's a snow day but it's only pouring rain in other eyes
No time off for the wicked or chemically enhanced
Your religion
My God
Your hate
My choices
Who made you a damn driven mad judge
Praise to the dealer
Praise to the pleasure worker
Death to the molester and murderer
Unlike customers seeking a service or product they desired
The dead and molested didn't pay for services rendered
So you know like a jigsaw puzzle we are broken pieces
But we can still match up perfectly as we lie down and you tell
me where's your stash

DROP CLOTHES & MOUTH WASH
(COUGH DROPS OPTIONAL)

Speaking in tongues when your words are worthless
Kiss or hiss it's all identical
Reaction noted but memory fades like a floppy disk
Play the Fool to fend off reality
Paranoid thoughts in a lucid environment
Trip through the cosmos colors brilliant
Yell through me I need your discipline
Cracked sidewalks with curbs crumbling too high to scale
Envelop me with your sarcasm blood dripping from your lips
Extend your claws and hold me tight
Let's go on a journey that might never end
Fly through the 133 planes of Hell
No Icarus fall of fault shall disrupt the adventure
Demonios everywhere with breath so foul
Beauty of the erotic grinding with promiscuous abandon
Stage of haze, sweat and lust mirrored by sins of the flesh
Outer surface of our bodies are just a statement of misery
Ropes of leather bound the thoughts of the mind
Morals gagged by satin sheets and Heavenly lubrication
Encounters justified after the fact
Dead weight cast away with no questions asked

EFFICIENCY OF THE GUN

Efficiency of the gun
Property of a whore
Naked sunrises dimly lit
Step past me as I fall
Crooked directions
Maps with no true destination
Wrong turn at the corner
GPS is PMS
Conflicts of your interest
Washes me away
In that high I seek
Burn baby Burn
Tag me on the toe
I've been dead so long
Everyone aware
Except I was the one who didn't know
Pistol grip in my hand
It's plastic façade so divine
The trigger of life
The hammer of numb
Thor laughs in my face
Knowing the weapon
Weak as Hell but still hell bent
Not an actual arm of fire
Lost mental state
Gunning myself to done
Termination of the soul
Nothing left

ELEPHANT IN A PLAYGROUND

Choices of life shelter the feelings
Your appointment as always three hours ago
Heavens gate just a block away
Turn the knob of emotional pleas
Step it up a notch to rupture the barrier
Where the grass is greener passage denied
Damaged separation with denial of the future
Butterflies flutter and bounce against the
hollow walls of your mind
Unconscious remains so vital you imagine they are aware
Dead and bloated ashes of loss
Meet the creeps that destroy your body
The mirror reflects them in your pupils
Spirits floating like a Ferris wheel off its axis
Stabbing your cornea with microscopic
splinters of hate and wood
Romance uncut with Satan handing you the roses of delight
Radiant sunshine emphasized your mind
In reality a flashlight in a back alley pointing you out
Things so close to you a few hundred miles away
Do a wrong then at your side for a split second
The contrast of life so jaded and wrong
Remember well and never forget
An elephant in a playground full of life
When angered the slightest move can exterminate
Modify and alter
Domino consequence
Change the roads others follow
Or perhaps putting them at a halting cease
Love conquers all but it didn't this time
Swing dance with Satan for 33 seconds
He's the ruler of the rhyme

EMERGENCY MEETING

Judgment shows no favorites out of spite
Heart broken in 103 pieces
The sky opens up to fly wherever Angels never dare
Admit the guilt then swallow the pain
Crowds rush for reality that's just a fantasy on the tube of lies
Staring at your crush but the emotions fall
to the ground inches away
Unheard, Unknown, Invisible
House of pleasure tainted with pain
Now crumbled with sand to its foundation
The rebar rusted with no strength to give
The sky closes with no love to show
Clouds turn purple with hail waiting to explode
Pound you back to the desert of your loneliness
Cactus shadows with thorns in your back your only comfort
Waiting rooms in a state of emergency completely full
You aren't the only one with a breakdown in life
Take a number and converse with your fellowship
Share the stories of confusion and dazed
with your tongue missing
Can't bear the truth but it has hit you full
face with an impressive impact
Knocked to the ground with the clique of the lonely and lost
Welcome to the club with a gun in hand fully loaded
Chamber ready to release and shower
fragments of your thoughts
Spread them out so they'll never connect again
Erase the pain and unpack your mind
Backup plan maybe just fly away somewhere far
Will God take down a plane full of nuns

With the hole I am in I believe so
I'll take that chance
Let the gamble of self-execution begin
Wish me luck

EMPTY BLANKET REVERSE X-MESS TREE

Happiness is our life
Or so we think
That next introduction
Could be our savior
Our guide out of this
Bodies warm next to each other the morning after
Or perhaps weeks later
Security our lock
Although constantly broken
That little tastes mends
Always repairs
Moves us into the next day
Knife in my liver
Etching of your name upon its handle
Giving the poisons another route to exit
Glorious Sunshine
Welcomes you or I into the next 1,440
Will we last or bow down before the end
Sweat drips from what still is tangible
My first or last breath
If this final dose of losing reality steals me away
Let me awake beside you if in Heaven or Hell
If there is an empty blanket next to me
My hand will be extended out hoping for your grasp
If even I have to wait an eternity
In my dark little corner with pinecone smells

FABRICATED ASPIRATIONS STENCILED IN FLESH

Present circumstances dictate the images
recalled from midnight liaisons
Heart pounding to the rhythm of a throbbing
encounter with juices to spill
Tension of another level riding a wave washing
away all sins for a moment of truth
Before it can be heard swallow it down instead of
spitting it out with a release of guilt
Lifeline to freedom being held in a swift vice like
grip milking it for all it's worth
Secret doors unlocked and open wide with sweet jewels of
treasure waiting to be polished
The ride of a lifetime transpires with recurring
authentic arousal
Eroding clouds of shyness making inhibition an extinct
confined feeling of the past
Pillow covered beds with sweat soaked sheets the luscious
roulette game you call home
One on one, two or quite a few mix and match the
combinations are endless
Comfortable in any situation with no points of interest
blocked by flashing stop signs
No boundary that can't be crossed with favors
of succulent flesh
Braced by a building wall as automobiles roll by with engines
purring your rpm to the red
Feel the abuse and drown in the stream of bondage rustling
your gear to an intense drive
You speak to God everyday when you touch your own
personal heaven
Oh God, Oh God I'm...

Leather masks and straps good lord you scream pass the rope
and bind it tighter
Emotional energy funneled through channels that can be
activated with a push of a button
Feel it rise its shadow a warm velvet blanket
wrapping you in warmth
Burn or be burned the game of life is never balanced
Detach the world and just crawl inside for the ride
Leave emotions at the door and go with the flow
lapping up the river
That carries desires, imagination, forbidden thoughts,
lust and carnal greed
Love is just a fantasy fabricated by evil itself
Reality is an unforgiving bitch with a bitter tongue

42
Don't listen to her voice
Words are crumbling boulders of doubt
The only bet that is guaranteed
Pleasure is in the flesh

FADE
(dedication to a friend)

He did all he could
From the day you were born
The darkness that resided in you
He was aware
Never stopped him one moment
From knowing what he knew
He loved you
You were his child
You were perfect in his eyes
An Angelic Demon
With a smile so bright
You were special in his soul
You were one of a kind
Rumors could flow
Night upon nights
Pointless hearsay
Nothing worth anything
Your charm captivated people
Despite what they assumed they saw
Or thought
Shooting stars
Did you make a wish?
I know someone did
3 wishes granted
Each one an Angel
In their own unique way
He loved them beyond death
Even though they had a
Sliver of demon coming from you
The reaper came

And I wish I could have stopped her
(I would trade places my friend)
The light of his eye did fade away
And I see those tears from your eyes
Roll down, down your cheeks
When you have a chance
Please open them and see
Three beautiful creations in front of you
They all have his soul in them
You will always be connected
Raise them well my friend
They are his Innocent Angels

FALLS OF DARK

Medicate me
Cure the disease
Dispatch the pain
Erase the hurt
It was coming for me
Stopped my heart
What do you want to do
Use me
Abuse me
Leave your mark
The curtain calls
Do your part
Can't you see
The situation is gone
Dusk has enveloped the light
I'm gone

FLOAT

Take me away from this
Release the binds
Step to my side
Allow my passage
The heat inside me
Clearness of expression
The transparency I seek
Effulgence of the Moon
Is all that I know
Days sleeping away
Nights wired awake
The ocean talks to me
Begging me to rest
Deep in her arms the cold embrace
She made me a promise
If my eyes should open
Upon her son she would place my being
Dry and safe on his lap with his father the Sun shining down
Gather myself with clarity
The Beach would wake me to a brand new day
His sister blowing the pain off my being
Chills on the surface of my flesh
The Wind carries the negative into the sky
So now I float
Maybe I can get it right this time finally
I'm enveloped in emotions
Wrapped in disgust
Chained with sorrow
Pasted with anger
Lined with hate
Injected full of doubt

Tired of running the course of life
Speak my mind
But it's never heard
Falling on deaf ears
I wait and wait
The eternity is useless
I pause for her sister the Moon
Take my views and observations
Lay them all out
Hope for the best
Rescue may be near
My fate in her hands
Now I float
And wish for the best
Float
Just let me float

FLOWER

Quagmire you left yourself in
Just too harsh to yield to in your open stupidity
Double the dishonesty of promises
High-pitched voices like Dino
Not the girls of summer
Whining for that next correct
Fact of fiction
But the tales of deceit becomes truth
The blemished gleam in your eye
Fog filled fallacies
Miry reconsideration
Nerves rioting for a peaceful fruitful calm
Morals debating and berating your dim conscience
Thoughts tremble like a crack baby coming down
Upward you fail
Flowing like an Estes rocket
Reaching for that rapture
Grab every God you wish to believe in
Lock them in your thoughts
Eradicate them with your last hit
Kill them with your overdose
They no longer survive
When your light burns out
A soul so dark it will never flower
It's seed is frozen below
Much too deep
Inside the betrayal of life

FOUL COW BLUES TO USE

An illusion maintained like a Barbie doll gone wild
Cracks in the sidewalk like the stuff in her veins
Solitude is her only friend
Like a Sasquatch with dreads
The deepest thoughts will never be found
Escape to where the bridges haven't been burnt
Crumbling artifacts of lies inflated
An archeologist couldn't decipher her past
Ravage the savage or abuse the meek
False insecurities stacked like boxes for play
Pathetic idiot with ideals that need to be shot down
Drastic plastic to compliment what's inside
False lies of self worth and the birth
Of matter in her digestive tract
Boo hoo why is she sad
The mirror might have been the answer
She has nothing to sustain

FRAGMENTS OF A MEMORY DISJOINTED BY A GUN ON THE SIDE

On the first day you destroyed it all
Hell hath no fury like a friend scorned but it has a spot saved
just for you
Saving the best for last but that's never good
Haunted freedom with bastard spit drying on the sidewalk
Three wrong choices result in negative tragedies
But what is it worth it to you
You'll never give a flying F
It's not your problem for now
Karma will reward you with the perfect present
While we laugh at your sorry dilemma
LOL x 333
Fuckers always get fucked back the essence of being
Maybe a few hour or days
Maybe a few years or decades
What comes around comes with blessed wrath
Feel the pain in your simple pathetic mind
Dialects of warriors just words without substance
Steal from the poor and die like the reduced and meager
You are no better than they and never will be
Big bang for the bucks that you pilfer
Although they are cheap corner firecracker pops
Flaming out with a flicker and 2nd hand smoke
Goodbye my love the rendezvous has ended
Black chrome eyes reflected by the gun in your hand
Trigger-happy blues your fingers twitch
Four walls, a floor and a ceiling your last friend
So many thoughts rushing through your anxious mind
Now scattered all over the floor, bed and wall

The investigators will never know the
fragments of your memories
Scattered and broken as they were in your skull
but they have opened wide
Disjointed and cooling for the world to see as the barrel cools
Nothing to see the sad fact of life
Loss for you and me

FRICTION OF ADDICTION

4 A.M. and the toll continues
Debt will never run down
The liquid of life fuels major arteries
The only sustenance to move forward
Soul rubbed raw the pain will never stop
Friction of addiction fluid needed
To stop the burning heat of a soul lost
A heart is a soul burnt with remains of resent
The house is never a home with memories in flames
The heart is a foundation with thunderstorms in it's closets
Secrets and lies to fuel the high we don't even know
Floating in space with the stars buzzing our ears
Far down below the Earth says hello
It's a distant gesture just to keep space
Our lies and destruction have ruined friendships
Decisions to leave are a must
Ruptured dreams and scattered thoughts in black
Time to leave on a one-way ride to close the deal
Grisly episodes of self-loathing and hate
Sacrifices to the fear of life
Death is the answer or so it seems
Puzzles of the mind with confusing questions
Another drink and then one more
Dive bars to airport bars
Strip clubs to empty hotel rooms
Home alone with a bottle in hand
Time flows with no resistance
Days evaporate quicker than the grains of the
devil in your throat
Tripping the skies to visit major cities
New adventures to ease the mind

Pour another drink hear it trickle
The story the same sure as the clock ticks
Ice cubes, the heart and time the constants in life
They can't stay frozen forever

GLOOM THEN BOOM

Explosions in your mind
Fireworks in your eyes
Sparklers in nostrils
Scorching the hairs of doubt
Flames in your ears
Melting the wax to seal the plug
Silence the truth
Invoke the lie
Flawed complications
Accurate warping cogitation
Objectives of desire
Disease of want inside your veins
Forgotten recollections buried deep
Clawing their way to the surface
Credit the scar
Debit the warrior
Beat the fool
Stake the island
That lurks in your head
Oceans of misery lap at your beach
Your ships seeking release
Sunk in the gallows
Of your mind
So deep
Warm bright waters slap your being
Swim away and the water darkens
Colder and colder with the further you get
Thicker and thicker your movement slows
Face your wickedness
Then ponder your path
Face the gloom you placed upon yourself
Last minute reaction
The gun goes Boom

GLORY, GLORY, GLORY HOLE IN MY HEAD

Rain pouring across the heart entrapped with
no way to escape
Speedway of the mind has no time for judgment
or understanding
Ethical concerns are valuable as pigeon fecal remains
Holy lasers and God created arrows from false Angels
the only familiar matter
Trojan horses filled like a piñata of goodies galore
Loaded veins more lethal than a weapon laden with projectiles
of hollow metal
It's about that time to move and step around the mess of life
Scourge of emotions swirl the thoughts once
straight and narrow
Turpentine visions and quaking nerves bottled inside
something synthetic
Your art project of life is a puzzle more complicated than a
broken Rubik's Cube
Interests in a free text from a supplier with sensational
motivations
All major credit cards accepted but cash is king
Tire tracks in the alley reminders of the marks on your arms
Each one represents the noise of the moment days ago
Party at 7:30AM with a crack whore boy who looks
better than your girl
Gutless reaction with movie star performance
all eyes are on you
Working it like race horse you pound away with a severe
passionate desire
Heart beating as you race to the sky zipping around like a
rocket man

Collisions of the Sun, mountains and oceans
quake your soul deep inside

Aftermath a mess worthy of a headache hours later
Bullet to the head the only solution producing fatal
results not wished for
For you, family and friends
Wish there was hope but you cashed those cards in years ago
Good bye my friend see you on the other side
Can we change places???

SLANG

Experience the White Crunch on your Blue Belly
pounding away
All Tweakend long
You Crank the Engine as you Speed down the Highway
Sip from your Crystal Glass gunning for the White Cross
20/20 clear vision in Hawaii on the boat at the Crater
Check the 222 address on that Chicago corner
Or skip over to the 417 in Missouri
Agua with Anny because the question always is
Anything Going On
Some Albino Poo for Alffy as you watch network TV
Let's jet set to London and see What's the Happening
Meet Artie down in the Atten Borough
Bache Knock or Rock the door with bag chasers
Running on high like a marathon looking for the Barney Dope
Baggers can scoop up the Batu with the Batuwhore
(maybe he is her pimp??? Hmmm…)
Her name is Bianca Beegokes and she is known so well
Times Whizz on by but it seems like you
have known her forever
A male Blanco Bitch showing off Bling inside a White Blizzard
Feeling the Blue Funk after being Bombed
by that Blue Acid you took
Booger bombs with a Philippino named
Boorit-Cubuano holding a bottle
Brian Ed's Buff Stick is Bugger Sugar minus
the Buggs & Bumps
Cuz the Buzzard Dust coats everything with a
high gloss sheen
A Crystalight night with a dash of Crysnax and
some Crypto Crunk

So you can Crow at the moon instead of howling
cuz you're jacked like crack
Heading to Creek Rock @ Sand Mt., AL looking
for some Cookies & Coffee
Cankistein Candy while on the sidewalk drawing
Chalk Dust cartoons in Pink
Hydro Hypes with Billy the Gemini let's Get
Geared Up and Go Fast
Gas and Gak with a Gagger in the bag doing the
wrong kind of Blow
Where is the High Speed Chicken Feed the
High Riders use???
I wanna talk to Gina tonight at her flat in Cali
San Francisco where the Pump is at to drain the
Puddle at Rudy's alley
Sam's Sniff of Satan Dust with three Sugar Sarahs
Proof in the pudding of truth accelerated
evolution is just a joke
Staying so arcane with Tweakers using Sketchpads
trying to be Spindoctors
The Neck Creature is Off the Hook trying to
Scout the Shadow People
In the end the Spinsters have a Sketch Monster Cookie
Even though the Toothless and Ruthless Speed
Freaks on P Head are Skitzers
Zooming in and out cuz the Bikerdope is so rock star WOW!!!
Billy once again looking for the Blue Acid down Chestnut
No such luck then all of a sudden…
(pause for 33 seconds)
Boo-Yah!!! Bottles on Haight Street Biznack the
demon offers his soul
Then he spreads his legs and gives up Cotton
Candy Crotch Dope

ChaChaCha on over for a lil Devil Dust or
Dandruff depending on quality
Torqued on Redneck Heroin riding the
White Pony yelling Who-Ha
A lil Whip for Tutu disperses the Ugly Dust on the Tubbytoast
Yeah it's Tish but what can you do??? Cri, Cri???
Let's trip the rift and find Choad to have
some Coffee, Cookies and CoCo
Zoiks it's time to Zoom to the Yellow Barn
for some Crizzy and Critty
Oh wait it's just the same like the triplets
Debbie, Tina & Crissy
Take a Zip line to Yead Out with a Yankee in search of Xaing
Twizacked by Chizel with Cheebah & Cheese
on Chicken while it's Flippin
Walk or Talk to the Crankster Gangsters while
they Criddle with limp limbs
(You know which one I mean…wink, wink, wink…)
OMFG they'll Cringe in front of the Cube
because there are Dingles in there Berries
Love is a Devils Drug that will make you Yammer Bammer
Burn you up from the inside out with pain
every hour increasing tenfold
Try to sleep but you continue to Wake next to
a Crack Whore so Crizzy
Looking in the mirror you see it's you with a
clenched Ratchet Jaw
Head back to the 415 and find Richie Rich to Rip & Rock
the Rocket Fuel
Poor Man's Cocaine but Project Propellant with
Dizzy D is Chiznad
Dizzle Dizzo likes to get Dirt on the Dirty Crunk Crysnax
Taking the B.A.R.T. riding the Rank Rails chilling
like Schlep Rock

Hunger from down under wanting Scwadge Scooby Snax
Smurf Dope is in fact really dope with a lil Motivation
She might be Chunkylove and Sprizzlefracked but
her White Junk is Shizzo
Can't get it up with the New Prozac in the
White House you are Sto-Pid
Let her Clean out the Chimney with a Tical to her
throat if are up for Zingin
Yay now you can Spin, Spin, Spin Sparked by a
Sparacked Speed Racer
Scattered and Tattered the White Lady says
We We We while Twistaflexin
Twizzles or Twiz oh Snaps let's go Ski the Sweetness Swerve
Bravo or Clavo my Chizel Chittle time for Sky Rocks of CaCa
Yama the Tweedle Doo while RumDumb is on
the Chank CR but no Dee
Talkie Time to the sky cuz the Spaceman is Spinning
with a fat Sack
Yank the Wigg while at Work along the
Way to a Whacked Shia
Spook the Tweezwasabi when trying to Peel Dope
Scante with a Smiley Smile taking a
Sniff of Vanilla Pheromones
Running Pizo while licking a Rosebud at a Truck Stop Special
Sliggers Toots but not the Reggae one while
Twacked Out on Tweak
Tripping the Trip beat up in
Shards and Shit by Shabs Shabu the Samuria
Spinny Boo Spinderella Squawks like Poop Powder Monkeys
Her Scap on Quarter Tea Bags with Quartz on
the Rocks Q'd to perfection
Quick to the Quill in her Powder Point Pootananny Sparkles
like Smack

It makes people say Ta'Doww Syabu WTF was that???
Tinkerbell on TIK going so high she can nibble on SpaceFood
Then float on down to that Rocky Mountain High
and chatter with Pookie
Stellar or Stallar Philopon Phazers are the Sha-Bang
I'm Evil and I'll possess you
Worse than the Tasmanian Devil on Tenner
Spun Ducky Woo to you and you and her and
that Fool on the side
Open your eyes
Your actions
Your addictions
Are that of an idiot
No hope
No funeral
Decompose into the sewer

GRANTED IDIOT

Foundations built on eternity
Dreams erected on storybook endings
Whatever you possess can never match
The next or the next after that
More beautiful or handsome
More young or seamless
More quick witted or compassionate
More curvaceous or toned
Lie to one lie to another
It's just the same
Words spilled regurgitated into a new ear
Complaints bounced what was once our home
Who was too busy
You are too dense to view
Look in the mirror
My time was yours as it might still be now
Dispute what I write but I saw it in your eyes
It gleamed so brightly speaking of another
That spark I recalled once upon many times for me
Hollow and empty is such an easier life
Whatever that can be grasped has no value
Blink of an eye it can disappear
Vanishing but leaving my husk of emotions
Cracking and drying in the Sun of truth
Broken hearts are usually never repaired
If it is the sick joy only lasts for a flash
Shattered again the impact is worse
Love is the most evil drug
Wish I never tasted it
My fault once again
For taking things for granted
Idiot

GUILT NOT WAITED FOR OR DESERVED
(The Final Poem Damn It)

My passion has dwindled streaming away like a
sparkler stick dimming to nothing
Repeated comments pounded into my corner with
nails of bitterness
I'm on your side but in simple times you never see
it or want to see it
Just around the curve I wait for you but you speed
by without a glance
Running on full steam you have a one track burnt
memories mind
Healing process will never happen but I
point to the sky and hope
That falling star is my wish every night and it always returns
Blame on others won't expand the solution ten fold or more
The solution is in you
Give yourself a chance
You opened your mouth and spewed the smoke
Let the poisons seep through your skin
Creep through your heart with barbed
wire legs spiders of disaster
Centipedes of destruction clawing through the
vessels of your brain
Licking and chewing your every thought
You'll never understand the damage you inflict more than
napalm on my soul
It heals quickly but scars eventually build so
what should I do after years of slight hurt
Stand by your side there is no choice for the
soul mate in my life

I need you more than you need me but maybe
I just don't see that
Two way mirror but we don't see each other
and maybe never will again
Birthdays ruined in the past I tried to celebrate
you but it was just an aftermath
Destruction of a soul, death of a smile,
funeral for a failure of fun

GUN RACK

Off the gun rack inside your head
Weapons of wit loaded with verbs of damage
A defiant gaze with a different shade of azure
Lonely and lost with venom to spare
Gasoline Angels coat your breath
Ready to ignite at the strike of a match made in hell
Diffidence of the brawn
Connective tissue and decomposing enzymes
Two sad peas in a fraudulent pod
Beacons of perplexity
Confute yourself with mystification
Sling the pain forward who stand in the way
Demi-God visions with judging eyes
The queen of apocalypse a legend in your own mind
Duct taped desires never concrete
Imagine what you will but the bond always breaks
Listening to nothing despite the roar
Your barbed wire needles strike with precision and force
Defeating those that pose a threat
You are the God of Death and Decay
Your imagination runs wild like a pack of wild dogs in heat
Running for her
The justification of your deceit
Ruler of the kingdom of dust
Your loose thoughts twist and fray
Stare with an intensity of a predator
Snarl with your hate
Deception of the sun bringing on a bright new day
Curse them for their positive thoughts of joy
Borders crossed or so you assume

You don't give a fuck and never will
Assaults of the tongue your surge of power
Firing with envy your gun is never empty
Bullets of bullshit explode from the jaws of an invertebrate
Spineless as you will always be
Inject the needle and float away
Your true face to society:
Useless

HISS HISS KISS KISS SUCH A BITCH

Hiss Hiss
Kiss Kiss
Turn your cheek but you are still my bitch
A cunt covered in so many palettes of deceit
The dick that you were chewing on was the dick that was you
Withered, decrepit vile and alone
Not even a centipede would let it's legs touch you crossing
your unconscious path
Quickly I skulk away trying to sneak past the misery you
protruded with a heart so cold
Vultures with wings dripping blood laugh like a hyena on the
most exquisite crack
Their back stabbing ways just a joke in my little black book
Each and every one of them will hand a paper over with your
name printed on it
Bygones will be bygones and they refuse to be your bitch
Little did they know they were the ultimate bitch
A splintered baseball bat and I detest that sport
Placed carefully in the rectum is the perfect tool for all the
tools that exist
Life is beautiful
Welcome as P.E. stated "To the Terrordome"
Downhill journey now from this point in time
Tick Tick...
I flick your eyelids with intensity
Wake the fuck up meet your hater
What? Your confusion thinks I should have said "maker"
Sorry bitch if I was your maker like any sane human being I
would have made a choice
Before the thought could have entered your mind in
destroying innocent lives
Abortion bitch
A rusted hanger should have been your only friend

HOLD

Aborted was the choice but not my fate
On hold since birth crying for something I know not
Waiting for life to explode into my face
Wash me with it's beauty
Drown me with sober dreams
Coins into the wishing well produce shit
Enough to write a book the adventure of lies
Mine or yours are just the same
Murky visions of excitement rendered dull
I'll never captivate you
Controlled for life
Never good enough
Too fat and thin
Too dense and quick
Trends in the magazines what the public follow
Obituaries are the place I should reside
The place I wake into every morning
Anthem of my motto: I am Dead
The job of life has laid me off once again
Drinking the hatred everyone spits on me
Ride the evil until I am spent
The bills of misery will never cease
In debt for eternity
My failure that I was blessed with
Born again like a Sabbath
Disturbing the priest and he still ignores me
Lost cause since the day I was born

HOLLOW DRIFT

Install the attitude
Projections of false spirit
Plastic wrapped dreams of ecstasy
Helicopter moons flooding the night
Stray from what you know
Snake tongues and rabbit feet
The promise of shattered smiles
Denial of sutures for the torn soul
In venom we trust
Inject it with a wickedness
Let the tidal wave sweep you away
Flood and wash your soul with warmth
Eventually the shell becomes cold and frozen
Flame up another
Then rise with the heat
Mellow melancholy nightmares
Hollow families with emotional riches
Valuable robberies of desolate hermits
Friends or enemies
Pick them well or so you thought
Temperatures approach the level of perfect
Numb bliss as you transverse the scenarios in your head
Was that creation worth it
Did their smile give you the highest high
Love never remembers
Pathetic thoughts only do
Drift away my friend
Drift

HONOR OF A WHORE

What could they have given you
Promises filled with rocks to drown you in the lake
Pipe dream love to the back of the cranium
Steak knife affection into your lungs
Arsenic tea for the heart so precious
Slicing your soul leaving lacerations for life
Love once known but now a husk of deceit
Knife in your back with a gleaming blade of falseness
My limbs are always open
The invitation to the dance in all of it's glitter
I'll lick you down every damn inch
Bottom to top
Side to side
Your perfect host of the tour
No one can do it better like the D.O.C.
Bent over backwards
You can invade my soul
Decline of the shallow pond you waded in
Drying up faster than a drought in 130 degree weather
No fault of mine
You choose your path of boredom
Suffer me not for your jealous ways
I am the one holding the cards with an upper hand
What hand I deal out to you is up to fate
Accumulate the means to gratify
Push the interest til the drops of wet come
Warm currents of the streaming consciousness
No refunds or loss on my guarantee
The Honor of a Whore
I will take you higher

HUMAN ATTRIBUTES FULL OF COMPLEX BELIEF

Manifestations of a soaped down body after an illicit meeting
Paper signs held up high so no one can listen in
Step but don't relax because Frankie is wrong on this account
Publish what you will but facts are always omitted
with vomit and anger
For your own protection the physical body can
only take so much
Forty-eight hour interrogation into the corrupt vessels and
organs proves too much
State of emergency the system is running below capacity
Run to the forest which is emerald at the spot 203
Green dreams of non-grandeur greet you with monsters &
monkeys
Staging a play with tricks of the mind art work
flooding the eyes
Explosive overload and heads held low the crowd watches with
curiosity
Describe the ride while six feet under
Go-Karts that fail every turn and straight away will
never keep up
Roller coaster of love or what you feel as such
Sensation of cause or is it just neglect
A cover story for the Addicted, High, & Always Broke
Move it over and let all systems fail with severe results
Setting alarms off but stealing money from our
children isn't in the picture
Pies with quality legs spread open don't know the deal
Tasty cherries and boysenberry delight with a wicked cream
Is your flat really a safe place to chill and relax
Tainted dreams and messed up visions are all the rage
Cheers and impressive quality with a grandfather clause

Reports with no quick fix
It's all a fucking maze no matter how oblique the view
Boo my friend
Reaper is waiting for both of us

I.D. WHAT???

Voyage of talks and dreams
We all have them but they just float
Foundations never built
Exercise of persistence washed away
Goals and visions drowned in the indulgence
The high for now is more important than the high for later
That eternal high of accomplishment
Sidewalks covered with mud and lies
Promises broken before the first words are spilled
151 and syringes are not the answer
Gin & diet
Crown & coke
PBR binges til twelve noon at the Double Down
Feels so good but won't dissipate the pain inside
Comments and snipes just ignore them
Discouraging thoughts burn so bad
Dark loss with stars burnt out
Substitutes for happiness won't cover the spread
Trying to keep that flame alive won't rescue your soul
The fire is fake just like everything around you
Douse the sickness then open your eyes
Friends will be there if you let it be
You need an I.D. for your life
Know who you are
And stick with it
Best wishes my friend
When you need me
You know I will be there…

IMPRESSION LEFT WITH A FORCE

Memories of thoughts drifted
Which would you take swiftly
Place it in the pocket of deception
Hide it like a thief in the night
One should not trust the world
Everyone carries a double-edged knife of tricks and lies
Imperial evil floats in the air
Like the smog of your purity
We were once free to dream away
Uncomfortable with each other
Now kicked out of heaven
Our behavior and ways have changed
Catastrophes of the heart and mind
Production of your own ruin
Blurry vision with luggage to match
Surrounded by the sea
Destined to sail for an eternal high
In the misery of our own creation
Although twin desires they run separate paths
You are in control and I have no say
Organic architecture of the mind crumbles and fails
Actors and actions well scripted
Unquestionable failure
Treachery in the smile we posses
Duplicity in the words we spill from a wicked tongue
Love will save us all
The preacher is mute with no volume
Preach what you must but it's dead air
Now love will kill us all
Misleading lottery to wonderful days and nights
Cash in our ticket and lose more ground

Footing never stable
Earthquakes and aftershocks disturb our foundation
Murder with slow hesitation
You're killing me and I want out

ISLANDS OR CONTINENTS

Choose which you desire
Solitude versus group therapy or what
Splashes of reality blood dripping down
No one to savor the pain that could be a choice
The next would be to share that high
Light it up and lick it away
Day to night then to dark of the heart
Afraid of the shock of the God that doesn't exist
Shuttered away enjoying your space
No prying eyes looking into your being of nothing
Safe and sound or so you feel
Still flying high again with nowhere to land
Reveal nothing to no one
Clouded in the crowds sway with the rhythm
The comfort of many keeps the beasts at bay
Yet they indulge in all you worship
False Gods at the altar that is so blurred
Visions of beauty only an illusion
Foundations of the heart were always weak
Submerged announcements pleading to be heard
Screaming and roaring inside your mind
Monsters and Angels fighting for your attention
Hand in hand they laugh at your lost spiraling path
Tracks of your life covered by a new layer of snow
Cold and frozen with winds to chill any spirit
Everyday is Halloween when we look in the mirror
Masks worn much and wrinkled with uncertainty
The lies have nowhere to hide from judgment
Hands shivering for a shank to plunge deep inside
The needle the device to take you to Heaven
Or could it be purgatory where all is numb

JOB TO BE DONE WITH FATE WATCHING

Fierce Mother wondering what the fuck happened
Sons & Daughters vanishing over time
Loss upon loss
Grief upon grief
Pieces cut then sliced to scrap memories
Pricks for friends swirling the typhoon disaster
People need help but eyes are missing pupils
Blind like goldfish flushed into the sewer
Resist the bliss but they could never
Returns and reruns a simple mode
Get it up back in the neck
Simple stab would end it all
That's what they wished for but chose the long way out
Dead dark night with glowing lights on the edges
Bloody noses and bruises just an appetizer
Arrested idiots with narcotics on the side
It still doesn't stop that someday
Phone call or the dreaded knock on the door
Why oh Why screams and bounces against the walls
One more time another one is leaving
Anticipation that lingers like a storm about to break
Knocked upon the side of the head
Trying to tune in back to reality
8 track tapes, VHS and Betamax
Death expanded
The Reaper loves everyone
Things lost long ago
Just as now

KNOCKING DOWN THE LADDER

The door to my heart was being pounded
Over and over again with racket
Veins on fire flowing freely
Surface of the skin in a glowing heat
Dripping like the slowest nosebleed
Most beautiful snow
Delicious numb explosions
Putting the turmoil to rest
Sweet candy kisses
Tingling touches of feathers
Sleep in my eyes
Kinetic dreams in my thoughts
Desire to float above it all
I was climbing the ladder to heaven
But it was knocked down from underneath me
Once again
By the destroyer
Myself

LANDSCAPE OF RAPE

I rape myself
Over and over again
Waters of my life flow
Drift away from me everyday
Taking the good
Leaving the debris
Further and further into the region of lost
My outline of life covered by delicate silk
Easily torn and cast away
The cuts are deep
The wounds have more depth
Self preservation not really
Destruction of the vessel
Fall or stumble
Crash and burn
Glide away to seek shelter
Once found set it to flames
Down to the ground in ashes
Mud filled pool
Stuck in a place that blisters with rejection
No where to go no where to reach
Hands like an amputee
No one can grasp it
So I fall
And I fall
And I fall
To the bottom
Dwell in the pits
Smell the disaster
Kiss the nothing
And beg for something
Release

LAST CALL FOR ALCOHOL WITH A LIL GLITTER DUST

Sneak peaks into the torn and tattered
Which way to fly not really a concern
Poke your eyes out with chili on your fingers
Feel it burn but it doesn't matter
True believer in that eclipse only you can see
A piece of what's left is rotting on the sidewalk
Car once owned burnt to a husk
Traded it off for a simple hit
Your sanity like a thug peckerwood so pathetic
Can't prove shit coming from a middle class or higher bracket
So lies upon lies flavored with barbecue bullshit
Tortured and abused those that you couldn't understand
Steroid bitchy boy with no intelligence
Begging for money now with fake intentions
Step to me and I laugh in your face you are nothing
Sweet home was the place you were loved
Now the welcome mat has been pulled, burned
and thrown away
I've got the last call for alcohol and drinks are on me
I spread the glitter everywhere for the true happy creations
Hugs and Kisses for Our Real People
Sad look on your face cause you can't get a taste
No one else laughs because they feel sorry for you
I laugh because you fucked yourself and so fucking deserve it
Enjoy being a bitch for the rest of your incarcerated life

LAST TUESDAY

Promises of sweetness
Holidays of Suicide
Joy dismissed
Esteem interrupted
What we view is clouded
Honor rejected
Love unfolded
Throats so raw
Quote my worth
In the negative
Let the rain wash me away
Aunties depressed
Uncles angered
Cousins confused beyond what
Music in the background
Loved ones in my thoughts
Ferris wheel of emotions
Roller coaster of life
Parents dismayed
Clyde moved on
So will I
End has presented itself
Done with it all
Last Tuesday

LEARNING HOW TO DANCE & THEN FLY LIKE A HUMMING BIRD

My oh my the choices we make
4 numbers picked in a lottery and they are all good
She's not your friend like Bonnie & Clyde
their foundation was tight
Car broken on the side with a temperamental
engine going for broke
Thanks for the tickets the show was awesome beyond words
Big shot with rocks and sticks can't compare
to what we need on the boardwalk
Face the music and reject the applause no one
is winning who supports the cause
Fool in the corner the room only has two walls
urine stenciled with tragic memories
Handouts of food and clothing the only true
income for an unwaged mortal
Ghosts inside the head knocking on various chambers
seeking to express discontent
She was your savior she was your ally she was
your personal chef's knife
Rear view mirror make up done so perfectly well
She denies everything but has more than a
million stories to tell
A singer for the neglected and compressed she
thinks she has values
A past particle of tread makes up the vast universe she sinks
into a black hole
Factors and hypotheses calculations result with a negative
impact always served cold
Floating on the surface of a liquid dream drifts you higher to
heights already found

Affairs of the veins open to anything and
anyone to pass through
Gliding on green clouds with purple bats
dropping tabs so colorful
Too young too old too thin too fat too lost too confused
Nothing matters in the end or the beginning
just the floating outcome
2 or 3 times a day naught a comparison to
what you actually do
Hit it seven times in 12 hours and it's
just a railroad of pleasure
Hold her hand but she only does that to share
Grinding and smashing she's showing you how to dance
Step, turn, spin, shimmy, pirouette and move away
Spread your tattered and torn wings

LISTENING AT THE KEYHOLE

Secrets whispered
Thoughts presented
Flowers wilting
Dwelling on the negative
Pondering thoughts
Losing paths
Words hidden in the wall
Doors sealed for the moment
Bed sheets wrap concealed hearts
Hidden deceit taps the soul
Corner bar waiting
No judgment placed
Dream well sleep
Wake the fuck up
Wishes of desperation
Victory with no hope
Circles of delusion
Prayers of loss
Get up
Get down
Get wicked
Get away
Return with no deposit
Nothing in sight
A wingless flat journey
Gravity the glue
Earth the anchor
Splintered boxes of wood
The perfect exit

LOCOMOTIVES & TANKS

Go
Stop
Pound down the hate
Relate to what has passed
Fury your thoughts to those that deserve
Barrel down onto those who plead
Innocent or what they claim
Pressure coming from the distance
Constrictions of their lies
Secrets as bad as any weather
Unpredictable
What happened
Can you remember anything
Collide with a dose of reality instead of LSD
Dazed and confused
But not really dealing with a seed
What comes to fulfill the void
Keep you here or so you think
Are they lined with gold and diamonds
Maybe with silver in a simple mans view
Nothing is actually precious
Looking in from the outside trapped
Inside with your tongue so wicked
Talking your maze
Twisting words to confuse
The person before you
Gives you their soul in a jar
Now you are trapped as well
From the inside looking out
No matter what
We all lose

MIRROR THAT

Purple posies float in the dawn of the remaining light
I think of her and smile
My flower princess
Will my dreams truly be Everclear lonely
The spirits fascination keeps me grounded
Like liquid pouring into a cup
Love knows no other destination but you
Clouds float beyond anything we can dream
The end is never and so are we
Corporation romances produced by movie star dreams
Fake beliefs that no one grasps with open hands
Feed us with the heavy they want to weigh us down with
Stronger than their ads we shall jump that mountain
Authors whose craft is the bullshit of presenting
the way to swing
Mess with the groove we won't break down
When it's wrong we know it's right or so we think
Bullets to the heart and soul burning with hot metal
fragments
Burn Baby Burn
Just passing through no rest stop for your emotions
Determined demon werewolves lick your senses
Weeping gently throw those tears of confusion away
Let them evaporate another time
She screams into my face
Professing the love that was never tainted
I close my eyes and hover
Grand reopening only for now
Eye to eye lips to lips
My tongue spills
Mirror That
x 333

MY OWN CREATURE

Instant surrender fed it the first day it stood in
my corridor of existence
Its dynamism was magnetic drawing in all the
particles of the universe
Followed me home with sad engorged blood vessels
in the recesses of its head
Hung around my dwelling hiding in the bushes when it wasn't
scratching at my door
Finally it broke ground and settled down in the tree house of
exquisite happenings
So I'll go and visit falling into deep conversations
that would last for what seems like hours
I'm so happy that it scares me when I come back down
2 in the morning like a surreal movie screen in black and
white project in the dark
Is it real or is it my creature playing tricks on me with my
hands tied behind my back
During the day no binding and the visions still manifest in
perfect clarity like HD
With the urge of the dark side it made me itch with an
irritation I could never imagine
In the beginning we played so much that
I missed it when it was away
An immortal spirit with unpleasant greetings if you don't do
things it desires
Hooked like a fish with a harpoon embedded deep in the heart
It reels you in licking at the wound and slowly consuming your
poisoned blood
Now it's in the doorway of my room an ever-changing
apparition

I close my eyes even though it's dark hoping
the black will consume it whole
Pitter-patter I hear the claws on wood clicking
towards me with a steady pace
Obstructions of the mind won't keep it at bay it
will always find a way in
Through the throat into the vein up the nose
the mind is a beautiful thing to abuse
Waking up as I wrestle with slumber trying to
break free from its demon grip
After the morning rain I see the rainbow with
an arc that is cracked
Once again my guard is down and it punched me
right in the gear box
It has me now I never could control it like an
unbreakable pimp
My own creature now owns me

NAMES AND TRAGEDIES

from artery to vein
The heart the first and last stop
Persephone the dealer that you only need and use
Her connections so well hooked up to your
personal well being
Pin cushions of the heart and mind developed
nerves so sensitive
Mountaintop views on almost every journey
Fly high and soar no end in sight
Serial killer of the soul you do it so well
Waiting for that ship come in to your empty harbor
It set sail so long ago never to return
Decaying pier holding your grotesque sanity
What would want to slip into your berth
Splattered euphoria that you can never share
Sushi dreams dice your morals into a faulty security
Bondage on the go your vessels scream
Tie me up for one more lick
Sorry for the other night but you really are not
Snuff the demons once again you hope
For that movie of your wretched life
Call my name it whispers in your ear
Although watching the clock it has all the time
Waiting with bated breath and a throat to swallow you whole
Desperation as you knock on the door inside your skull
No one is home but the urge is there
Banking on withdrawals with queens and kings of deception
Illusions of the hand and tongue your personal debit card
The people and names you'll never remember
The tragedies you left in your negative quake
For you or they
There is no perquisite left

NATURE TURNS FROM YOU

Compassion reaching its apex directing the wrong
Hustling the hyenas of your last place habit
Adduce the information to those that pity
No walking that thin line between pleasure and emotion
Erased so long ago you can't follow it back
Consuming the fragile character of delicate souls
Situations continuously shifting through time
Key of adaptation held in your shaky claws
Absent ceilings with no limits to your high
Black purple horizons paint the landscape of
your secret portrait
Contours once of love and devotion now filled with distress
S.O.S. to your self treated like a signal that
was silent and unheard
Echoing against the eardrums of the deaf
Redesign the faith you once had with an appearance of calm
Land filled lies of a train twirling off its rails
into the sea of the dead
Currents capture and drag you beyond what withstands
Persuasion of the innocent your craft at hand
Bellow the magic of your wit and deceit
Scoring pebbles from a stream
Instead of the treasures of an ocean of reward
Everything changes the world
Energies negative crumble and destroy the canvas of life
Hold me tight your arm conveys to the tourniquet
The cribs that held you once as an innocent
thing are memories gone
They are now the place you seek to equal the
house of lost love
Holding hands with that vice grip elevation

Feel the rush for a few minutes but it's good enough
Closet under the stairs your secret place to escape
The excessive doghouse deep below
Where your human nature is buried

NEGATIVE THOUGHTS

The paper plates of my mind are as flat as
your emotional product
Your thoughts are just full balloons of helium lies
The installation of hypocritical self medication has no use
Yes the use in this stupid hallucination
Heart pounding away with death at my door waiting
for the lock to break
Motivations of all things treasured
Just a blank slate on the cracked wall with
dreams erased in the distant past
A quarter in your cup
Won't fulfill what's been missing since the third day
The silence of three dildos crammed into your orifices
In the end you are just like the masses sharing the same gene
Chromosomes numbered 19-20-21-16-9-4
Translation:
STUPID

NEGOTIATING COLD CLIMATES
WITH MASSIVE DEBT

Superior variety of chocolate morsels for the souls
Strawberry dipped in mouth melting confection
as the heart ceases to beat
Flat line on the Highway to Hell AC/DC knows so well
Decisions display consequences but true Fools never ponder
Issues and grievances left ignored with a shot of JD on the side
Comets streak but never show their nether regions
Although they fly across every aspect of Earth
Eyes sewed shut with fraying rope
Trapeze artist with the poles to ground
Trampoline net outstretched with spider webs of deceit
Black widow dreams on LSD
Choose your poison but beware of the server
Crack in your lips hide the Moon and the Sun
Misery that once was ecstasy with a bump
Masking ulterior motives works every now and then
Stars shine like a spotlight on our flaws
Cracked facades with caked lies covering what
can't be explained
Trust was lost 333 miles ago with that broken tool
Save my life and we may illuminate
Wasted thoughts on wasted wishes
Whoever ODs first is the one to lose
Snatch what is left and invoke
Eyes roll back with puffs of air
Blinding your thoughts a sea of beautiful madness
For a moment we exist in each other

NEXT CORRECT

Let me marshal the resources inside my mind
Crawl and look through every broken door
Demand what I want
Then collapse to the floor
Give in to temptation
Let my liver bleed
Your soul to keep
Is not mine to harbor
Traveling the same path
We have seen each other more than once
A slight nod
Nothing more
We pass each other in routine
Searching for that
More
More
More
Beading drops of sweat
Sting my eyes as I wait
For that next high
That next correct
Hoping for something to ease my thoughts
Crashing and breaking
A familiar dark alley
We bump into each other
Unfortunately
Not with coke
Our physical bodies
Our eyes and empty souls done with this
They seek not freedom
They seek bliss

NIGHT OWLS IN FLUFFY PINK & EARLY BIRDS IN ORANGE FLANNEL

Typewriters at night prove to be a fatal flaw
Drawing and consuming the soul with no
chance for redemption
Destruction of evidence with an O.I.P. (Operation in Progress)
100% death proof with a dark soul at hand
Warrant to search the premises of whose mind
are we dealing with
Yours or mine or maybe that girl over there
Lost in thought and dazed as usual all generations are doomed
Lack of sleep provides a litany of fantastic side effects we'll
never comprehend
Confidential doors are now wide open like at a swingers club
Burning with desire but the wrong one
that would invoke salvation
Improving one self is a permit with a stamp to get back in
Informants & confidants turn you over like a roasted pig
Spilling guts and hope accounting for your fabrications
Try to manage a surprise to feign the guilty
Worn out like a vibrator with dead batteries
but still pulsing to go
Sleep it off then do it again with some flare
Shag covered head rests kept your skull comfortable
Phone calls ignored
Doors un-open despite the knocking in your head
My oh my
Conceivably
Better off Dead

NOT LIKE YOU

Not like you
Perfection doesn't exist
Blurred and hazy December morning with fog gripping the
views once beautiful
We all have a chance to save ourselves but our nightmares
propel us further away from the exit
Proud of the pain dampened inside souls charred and weak
Selfish with lust with money to burn made
anyway possible knees to the floor
Our souls at their mercy or so they think
We bloodied our hands and squeezed out the last drops of
blood from our hearts
Beliefs in Gods won't help our cause so we put them at fault
Stealing smiles from close friends now their backs are turned
Their hands amputated no longer free to give
Chances abused with no gun to our heads but the
imaginary one of self-hate
Barrel smoking with a lil substance dripping off the end
Revolving around ourselves crucified with
implications and terror magnified
A winter storm is never calm but cold and full of hate as
Mother Nature dictates it so
All over the universe our minds wander our craniums unable
to contain ourselves
Swing or walk this way we'll always share unless
there is only enough for one
Flesh, product, insanity or words all are up
for use, abuse and sale
With Suicidal Tendencies we have a Monopoly on Sorrow
Craning our heads left and right and to the back
wondering who is that???

Just the ghost in the mirror of a beautiful past
that was once so innocent
Mental fixations on a sterile barbed wire hook
won't cure the diseased and lost
Distressed lot of Fools questing for a failure as
they spin on a merry-go-round
Waiting it out some can easily beat those insecurities
that grip our minds full of disillusion
Others like us can't deal with it and take the eject button out
Sleeve full of memories that even the deaf and dumb can feel
Walls and ditches and barriers every which way we turn with
no escape that we can become loose and free
Influenced by stupidity and hate trying to prove we
belong as a member of society
The world is a stage and our acts are just a simple bluff to get
to the next red carpet leading to bliss
A slate that's a puzzle which we can't wipe spotless
Too many jagged edges and incomplete pieces
that will never fit
Stumbling for the next fix gazing out of the
window on Lombard & Steiner
A view to embrace but that doesn't matter because
everything is transparent
Struggling to be aloft is the only situation at hand
Our biggest secrets are the ones we think are
hidden from concerned eyes
They all know we reside in our cabin of demise

NOT SET UP AS A JUDGE

Introductions to creation minus options equal instability
Surprised by failure: request, solicit, beg, entreat then shrug
Rain drops smash down like 3lbs water balloons
exploding at every step
Phone numbers that ring forever always a disappointment
Under a microscope all the repulsive information is
blooming with dour light
Hammer with a wire can't smash or strangle that
nocturnal flower
Taking care of business but its never completed
just flirtations with demise
Getting to London on the F-train and a good ole
girl twitching for a fix
Flat screen reverie and you're dressed in a robe with flip-flops
3:00AM arrives and the living room becomes your final stop
Thief in the night you are only ransacking
your deteriorating mind
Lying awake night after night the way back is an
uneven, unlit wretched path
Would of, could of, should of but never I did it
Breaks a rare occurrence with mad certainty so
don't set yourself up
Judge, jury and executioner
You'll never be the mentioned above
Just a victim of your own crimes

PASSCODE

Tears burn holes like acid venom in my world and heart
Midnight hour or perhaps 3 hours past
33 minutes Purple and black bruises accented
with glowing green
Step into my parlor and feel my pain
Beating rhythms repeat inside of your mind
Shallow costumes with deep regrets
Long showers of rain pulsating on the ground
Tears of Angels who lost the contest to lead me out
Stepladder to Heaven full of splinters and terrible lies
Demons below lashing out with claws worn dull
Too many sinners for them to retrieve
Flesh stripped away slice by slice
Empty unpleasantly cold and tasteless
No flavor to offer when what lurks inside has no life
Profound sorrow with an injection of anguish
Losing grip as I gun for the last minute clutch
The key for escape rattles to the floor
Like old bones riddled with myeloma
Creaky and brittle a mirror of my heart
Circle of Fools waiting for me to return
Don't cry for me it was my option
Eyes fade to black lids shutting down
Cyclonic winds spin me around and around
Tumbling faster than anyone lost in Wonderland
Rock bottom I hit where I bow down
Rise again wearing my crown of dirt
This is my domain
I own my hurt

PERHAPS PASSING TIME IS A BEAUTIFUL THING

A premiere of the missing and lost wouldn't attract a crowd
Bits and pieces stolen over time slowly rot the soul
An author of lies and deceit
Friends used and abused like the $5.00 friendly lost whore
House to house looking for an answer
Holy drinks with some bread on the side
Pray for a return on all the heart & soul laid out
Hoping they are found and wishing for a miracle
Miracles happen but rarely for the good
Always shafted and left for dead
Letting time pass might be good for you
I'll hold your hand

PROPER AND TWISTED

Step into my room
Let your thoughts drift and sway
How are things Sugar Plum of the castle in the sky
With a Black and Purple fly whispering into her ear
Telling her how to protect the view of life
Do you dare
Do you try
Christmas trees rejected but always a gift
A little light shining on you despite the gloom
Silver lined clouds with platinum bonuses
Must be Heaven or something like
Addictions of the soul are so hard to mend
Yet that addiction is the sweetest taste
Hours, dates and minutes made the Goddess I serve
Numbers and records make the dream
1st is the thought of your beauty that numbs me
2 past 17 your body breathes with wicked lust
Like Black Flag 1961 is the perfect year for
people with strong ambitions
A.M. is the best time to answer the phone 702-460-***1
Purpose in life not to receive enticements of the flesh from she
Pleasure her beyond belief is the only ambition
Turn to the side and ride the perfect moon
Pound for glory or redemption but do it hard
Move with fury and passion all entangled
Flesh sliding against flesh so well lubricated
Pink and Green Dragon flies buzz about your head
Guiding you to that high that can no longer soar
Heaven achieved you are there
She is all that you wanted and desired
All that exists and what is real
She is the addiction of all addictions
Nothing else compares

PULVERIZE THE LEVER

Smash it
Kill it
Destroy it before the sun sets
On another dried concrete curb with blood the
only answers to existential lies
Dreams and lies extinguished like an after thought
Depression flowing like speed dragging it deep
Sinking to the abyss with no air pocket of freedom
I know who I want to take me home tonight
It's not you because I'll bury you beneath the
concrete pool already built
So far below that the sun can't even decay your rotten soul
Yeah mother fucker who do you love
Never was me
Here's my middle finger step off
The glass that encases all fabricated memories will shatter
tonight
Vanished

PUPILS THAT GRADUATE TO A COFFIN

One thing not counted for its reliability and perfect record
A self-murderer or is it a just a murder of your
own soul inside the cage
The mind is a wonderful thing that can
conjure up wicked thoughts
Bloodlust, heated passion, inviting passion all evaporate
Praise to caution and the misguided souls
intercepted at various paths
Headaches with earphones the whispers amplified beyond
anything imaginable
First class postage and hysterical requirements
indicate a slight smile
Your eyes were so wide open to engulf the world
Dilated for a long spell in time now they are blind
Close them my friend and sleepy well

RECALIBRATE THE WALK ABOUT THROUGH THE ALLEY

Shuffle and glide with no cares in the world
Back street or bike path next to the lake
All the same damn shame
Bad medicine with a little flavor on the side to
make the taste so good
A perfect person with lies flowing to the top of their cranium
A sour explosion with sweetness on the end to tempt the fool
Asp vicious bites with snake like quality
Why do the dogs bark when there is nothing to fear
Loud voices in the dark projecting transparent movie scenes
Illusions or insanity that cross the vision of our eyes
My, my, my we are losing it
Waiting in the doctors patient room images float
Wild scenarios that you can't believe but they exist
Another reality or are the meds wearing off
Habit of routine doesn't explain the wicked descriptions
The ones that your eyes convey to your confused mind
Maybe there are holes in our head from too much E
Filled up from another reality trying to cross over
The laughter in your head tells you there are no worries
Another episode of lunacy and the prescriptions
are still not working
Swallow down the fear and call yourself on your phone
Imagination running amuck but your voice
tells you it is not real
Lets get connected before we die
Feel the pain and then let it go far away
Set our souls on fire then swim in the oceans of our emotions
Where we can feel the calm we never knew
Peace
Tranquility
Numb
Normal again maybe

REFLECTIONS

User I confess with a hint of sincerity
Born that way it flowed in my blood
Like oxygen for the lungs a natural gift
Melody in the mind or so I thought
That sugar sweet song was basic taste
Foundations that sway in the wind of life
So many that have crumbled but I resurrect
The stupid clown who smiles with no knowledge of calm
Keep traveling a path with no right but plenty
of smiles and wrong
Escapades of ecstasy with close quarter touching
Another track and looking to win
Smells like shit and it's not the horses
Scabs infected with sins of disciples past and present
200lbs Demon with a syringe beats the Angel down
Monkey on my back the cousin of the clown
Laughing at my stupidity I'm it's puppet
Fist up my ass it makes me speak in tongues
Words I spill are what you and everyone wish to hear
Lies of the Adder fuel my influence
Stories written and told with structures of idiocy
I'm the best at it no minor cracks to lead to my fault
Hidden gems lurk in my mind
Although the holes in my matter let them escape
Fly Fool Fly you never know
Height is not reality just a description of being
Rock bottom is reality and we're not talking about La Brea
Tarred and feathered rolling in my Eldorado
Faster I travel like the Jetsons
You are stuck to me in the black liquid goo
Oceans of shrooms our only life boats

Once floating now we sink
Down
Who the fuck am I you ask with presumptuous snarl
I push you back and request that you finally focus
I'm your reflection

RELIC OF SKIN

Moving to a lower level
Fucking with me blows the deal
Soul already sold but now invalid
Not even worth a pebble the size of my heart
Advanced necromantic ways
Board materials speaking to the dead
Forceful reunion developed in the seed
Examples of lust that has faded away
Scriptures that have been written never the truth
Sweetness soured to lemon drop love
Dialects of the tongue silent as a fools bright idea
Flickering with matchstick illumination
Quickly to flame out
Lofty goals with gutter sewer dreams
Kiss the boot of ruin with bile on the side
Deity or joker all just the same
Mortal decay with Goddess perspiration
Pollution of the body yields to failure of the mind
Peeping into the ingestion of the caverns of the spirit
Black dark caves rocked with thoughts moving in a slow roll
Up and down, side to side the waves glide with fluid precision
Destiny a glimpse with shattered binoculars
Spider web walls lined with sticky announcements
Look to the sky and spread your arms
Accept your exquisite sins
Sleeping with the Gods
Licking the Angels
Jerking the Demons
Catastrophe has never been so saccharine

REROUTE THE LEGS THAT SPREAD

Not the legs that spread that cause the disruption
My own thoughts of sin and sex and lust destroying
Love lost beyond any redemption
Fool at the altar begging for a miracle
Forgive me for I have
Fucked up as any human would do
Placing myself as a train would do in a perfect
couple of the latch
Unions joined but only for the run be it short or long
Part ways then hook up once again with another rail
The white makes it shine so beautiful
Mixed emotions of cumulative hanker desire
Round and round I spin and stumble
Falling to the open arms of the hunger of orgasm
Plow and surround with ecstasy doubled
Tripled if a friend or fiend was there
Curled up inhaling the night while reflecting wisps of smoke
we weave the flesh
Grind and move with passion and lost love
Intimacies with bleak returns
Whatever sacrificed is always nothing gained
I want to remove the thorns rooted in the
nymphomania of your mind
But when I do I'll venture to the next open lips to proclaim
emancipation
Together releases or forever separate and free
Hunger of the whore
Salvation of the slut
I am my creation
You were a stop on the way

Mutual desires with diverse feelings
Poles apart contrary to the heat
I bow down and accept my defeat
The enemy is me

RESSUREKT, DESTRUKT, INSTRUKT

The fall of liquor
The liquor I lick
Brings me back to life
All that I missed
Fountains of alcohol
Fountains of life
Here and now
What
I thought
Eyelids heavy with gleam
Alive once again
Back with a calm
Smile on my face
Pleasure embroided
Stitches in soul
Sutures of the false
Dead silent calls
Repetition in a spiral
Same thing as last year
Put my foot to the brake
Squeeze the handle
Stop this ride
Little too late
Organs fail
Include my heart
Push it forward
Only one more drop
Failure everywhere
The liver is rejecting
Soul denies
Ghosts of friends fade away

Floating somewhere someplace
No Angel to save me
Fucked for the last time or so I think
Bow my head in my own defeat
Don't follow my footsteps
I ask you from my heart
Be strong and follow your visions
Your soul is stronger than you think

RESURRECTED LIKE A DEITY

I'm your friendly neighborhood lost fool
Public property the idiot slut
Open to ways
Not just your way but anyway
Emotional loser
Never confident when sober
The demon child
Devious thoughts within
Side street
Back Street
I'm your personal whore
Drama queen
The deaf man heard me
Scream like a bitch
Turn about is fair play
You or me
Wait
Switch
Truth to and fro
Superfuckingcagafuckinglistic
My eyes are open
So why aren't yours
Tread on my path
Then tell me which way to go
I'm not a follower
Blind and drunk is the way I walk
Let my hand go
Pretend not to see
Music is my savior
Gossip on and on with your babble
Closet of your lies

Trapped inside
My own fault
As to where I crawl
Nightmares strangle me
Asphyxiated by my own pillow cases
Abyss of fiction
Angel of broken dreams
The emperor of Nothing
Crack in the sidewalk
All can step upon
I am all that is never envied
Never strived for
A false idol of deceit
Look in the mirror
It could be you or me

REVERSE THE SCENE UNTIL YOU NEVER KNOW

Awkward instances as we sat next to each other
Slowly changed when we felt the injection of paradise
Ignorance was more beautiful from the brutal truth
Buttons of highs moving a step to the next level
Unsnap the fronts and all will show
Down the path so well traveled
Omens for advancement into spiritual joy
Illusions and perfect happiness hold their hands together
Accepting the considerate with blood stained arms
Assassinate the body with deputies that alter
everything and all
Prison time isn't an alternate version for the
mind to think about
Locked in your own cell for ages and eternity with an extra
day tacked on
Questions for the right arm but the left is willing to share
Arguments for reality blur the lines of what was once insanity
Mornings of tomorrow pushed too far into the future
Persons of interest are no longer interesting or a relief to see
Unless a product in hand that is willing to be
shared comes with the view
The distinct consciousness that once burned so
brightly years ago
Darkens like the morning Sun on a bleak cloudy day
Torture, twist and bind equals slight relief
Bruises and blood emotions so limp
Self doubt like a mailbox with its lid open for weeks
Invitation to steal your character tattooed across your forehead
Contracts with the Devil and demons inked on skin
Track marks dotted with periods for emphasis
Life a tragic comedy with constant laughs at your expense

Embark towards horizons that will shatter upon touch
Whispers and screams from conspirators and lovers
Move on my friend let us find the next blemish
We'll never know who left the mark and stained our soul

RUSTED HALO

Slipped from your head
Crown once proudly worn
Chokes your neck
Strangles yours goals
Barbed wire soul
Razor blade grin
The innocent Angel
Now an empty traitor
Secret passages
Through the back door of your mind
Touch of light dims by the minute
Darkness fisting you so hard
Demolition your movement
What you seek shall destroy
Wings plucked of feathers
Prevented from reaching that true high
Liquid jumping from the depths
Dragging you back down
Simple ease of an inconvenient crutch
Keeps them spread for all to see
Flightless with cinder block emotions
It doesn't matter where the halo hangs
Even if it falls to the ground
It can always be placed back
Yours can't
It's rusted beyond repair

SCATTERED PUZZLE

Shooting star wishes inside the polluted needle of your syringe
Society and it's trip wires keep you in a collapse
Emanating smells from a decayed heart
That once pounded like a bitch in heat
Jigsaw puzzle disaster
Senses of tomorrow scattered everywhere
Lost in the confusion of thought
Should I stay
Should I go
Why can't I be like they
Dead emotions prep bitch fake
Confusion of your thoughts reinforce the maze
Love once lived
Emotions that have failed
Coyote eyes burn bright in the desert of your mind
Scouring for that release of purebred lies
Dreams of the dead
Gone long before your eyes opened
Wake the fuck up and see why you are here
The life you exist in isn't your home
Born and breathing but it's just a visit
You are not here for the long run on planet Earth
Treat others well then say goodbye
Information of the heart corrupted and invalid
Canyons of your mind echo with history
You wish you could rewrite
Just a cur to the popular and shallow
Fur so dreaded and nappy
It's a dog's life
Tampons in a toilet the only truth
They left you bloody, wet and useless

SCUFFLE WITH A TROLL THEN YOUR DEAD

Three Fools at the bar
Sipping their intoxicants and wisping smoke
Second hand but most likely the fifth or seventh
Instigators and traitors they are all the same
Bull shitting losers who will betray you in a minute
Gave you more love and respect then any blood member
of your family
Keep talking your shit and walking that stroll
my misguided troll
The ugliness you see in the mirror is exactly
what you possess inside
Wretched and without any divine merits
You are the true loser with cancer in your heart
Think you are a player but you are not that clever at all
Knew of your game since day one and now
you wish to torment me
I show everyone love beyond words and you play your games
Go on and run you little troll so hiding under
your insurance scam bridge
I'm the God of Fuck and will fuck with you now on and on
Leave well enough alone and all have would been good
Now the greatest reality show of all time will be in your face
No mirror to mask your pathetic decay
Send all the letters you want you have no proof
you jealous monster
Keep your thoughts to yourself
As for mine will eat you alive and regurgitate your
meaningless remains
I'm an Angel to many and a Demon to a few
Now I am your personal Demon and I'm ready
to make life new

Suffer you
Suffer me
What's lost is your stupidity
I'm now your best friend
Destroy all you believe in
Fuck with an Angel
Are you that stupid
God is always on my side
Created miracles and saved lives
Stay under a bridge as I ruin yours
What a beautiful life
My name is Dust

(SELF MEDICATION OF AN IDIOT FOOL)

Low self-compassion
Furious Faster Quicker
I'm a simple mirror for the sun
My brightness outshines all the negatives
In all it's glory our relationship is temporary
Tomorrow's sorrow is packaged in aisle 17
bottom left next to the bottled cherries
Eight Balls and Fairy dust
Swish and twitch then thrash with abandon
Fish out of water gasping for life
Baited by lies yet you still bite
The hutch will always be a bitch
Storage of memories lost and lies brooding
It will use everyone that crosses its path
Mirror, Mirror on the...
We always fail and fall
Predicaments of a reptile
Lounge in the Sunrise of my mind
Bask in the warmth as I stare at your Cold
Your witchcraft is so clever
Fooling a blind mob with hatchets in hand
I'll sic and attack you with my fog sickness so thick
Lick you to death as the moisture wraps around you
Suffocating breath
Brutal Demon
Seductive Siren
Androgynous Angel
Gruesome ghost
I'll chase falling stars til the sky is pitch black
There may be a chance of hope still yet

Even with a sponge soaking in the ocean
You can't produce a single tear with blood shot eyes
Ranch dressing with chicken and fries
Voodoo spells and greasy lies

SHRIEKS AND PEEKS

Goodbye to the fear and book of lies
Lullabies for the babies of your personae that cry everyday
Wallow in your shit stained dreams
The diapers of your life hold your self worth
Never change them and the lower you fall & fail
Disciples of the dance with a demon in hand
Kiss the hand that feeds your wicked need
So weighted like an obese corpse
Sinking to the bottom of your rotting truth
Secret lives of the hidden, desperate, young and gifted
Frightening and fascinating haunting treasures sealed inside
Entice the stupid and lure the weak
Constrictions of dreams
The pursuit of what you'll never seek
Laugh at those that pass
But the last is on your pathetic self
Stories written of the road well traveled
Yours is nothing born again
The same old heart pounding song
The path used so well worn
Shriek like a bitch but the ghosts will always peek inside
Haunting you forever for the lies you tell yourself
Sick & trembling and shaking like a pup in a freezing wind
Innocent and lost with no clue where to go
Judgment served always the one pitched forth into loss
Wallow in the mystery with no answer of value
Testify to the Heavens with no reply
Kicked to the curb where we all belong
Useless and wasted nothing new
Pathetic and worthless
Cheating yourself

Sunset dreams will never manifest
Dead in the night heart stops cold
Eyelashes burnt back with the flames of lost trust
Nothing inside that's real so they turn to ashes
Trust redefining that it was never valid
All lies and pan handle wishes
Raven wings with kisses on each cheek
Pull my soul up and away
Leave this mortal coil as empty as I feel
Move
Move
Fly away
Dozens of lies within your dynamic mind
Let me leave them so far below without a hint of guilt
Your high pitched tales of love were vacant
Elevated sweetness on clouds that never floated
Now there are thunderstorms inside
What the Hell am I
Nothing
Always and forever

SITUATION POOP

Hands tremble as I snatch your cell phone
You don't know I did and never will
Scrolling through the messages looking for proof
Lies and denials
Flirtations and lust
Images of negativity with sprinkles of doubt
Wayward ways on the roads less traveled
So many people yet they never really count
Trust was never an issue but now it's a question
At times it seems you are miles away
Yet just around the corner of my mind
Once plugged in now a possible break in connection
The wrecking ball of love shatters all hope
Bat out of hell looking for Heaven
Freedom and closure is what I seek
The path my emotions pound upon is most likely a lost cause
Yet I move forward because you are there
The most precious treasure I may never delight in
Models of morals we both possess
Shoe box dreams push the confusion
I wonder of your choice and route
Dark clouds of deceit wander my jumbled thoughts
Your smiles and attitude with those you say are beautiful
Push me aside because I never get that reaction from you
Push comes to shove I'll just fall down
You can't make any person fall in love with you
Addicted to your soul and love I am looking into the
headlights of your mind
I hope they will always shine down upon me
Head bowed I replace your phone
No evidence of betrayal
I am sorry so deep inside I didn't trust you
I feel so poopy

SKY-SCRAPING LUNACY WITH A TWIST OF LIME

Names never given but faces remembered and rejected
Extreme foolishness and a joker with jack to the side
Fleeing from tears with nowhere to hide
No matter where you go the soul contains them
Drops of lime touched sadness waiting to pour
The rabble inside the mind like thunderstorms of lost souls
Engineers of our core can't construct a barrier for emotions
Conspicuous and seedy with twisted minds
that speak no matter what
Found something and it wasn't inside but a
little over left of center
A committee of central souls parade around the
head like a thrilling carnival
Rio De Janeiro with a lust for millions and more
Ministers on the dance floor sitting on
their couches of comfort
While we spin and dance as if nothing else matters
for now or tomorrow
Toasts and boasts, slander and rejection,
hate and love, envy and lust
All of it mixes well into the concoction of
life with a twist of lime
I'm yours
You're mine I hope
Let's touch the sky

SNIFFING THE CALVARIUM

My words are just clouds
Scattered throughout your memory
Once in awhile they rain down onto your thoughts
You remember for a moment in time but
Instead of flooding your mind they evaporate
The cracks in your heart sip the blood of others
Opprobrium actions with false aid
Arrogant wars of your distorted personality
Discomfited disciples would never walk at your side
Tossing and turning with fury and disgust
Twins of despair invoking nightmares
Just sleep it away by morning it will be gone
You have become your own devil
Your presence will stir the innocence to flee your mind
Tornadoes in your veins wreaking havoc
Miracles lurk in that syringe you tap
Scrambling with fluid fury attempting to
escape out of the needle
So that the Gods and Spirits will be granted their wish
They want to converse with you
To reach that ultimate high you have climbed
mountains of bones
Leaving the dead behind to taste that critical moment
Expand the darkness to invert life and death
Your shadow now lies in front of you
Pointing to your direction in life
Death warmed over with flowing robes
You carry it like royalty
Not on your back or shoulders
But upon it's throne perfectly balanced in one single hand

The canyons of your mind echo history you
wish you could rewrite
A jigsaw puzzle disaster clearly defines the crooked
lies being born in you
The gremlins and goblins represent the monsters inside
Sniffing at your skull waiting for your mind to rot

SPINNING CONFUSION

World is spinning watching my existence
through binoculars laughing
Knowing I haven't learned a damn thing
Fences are the barriers in my thoughts that separate the
happiness and depression
Keys in hand will jet me down through the pathway
Strung out on dreams that will never occur
in my limited future
I look in the mirror and make a wish
Step up close as if like James Brown I'm going to kiss myself
Breathe on the glass surface then write
my name with my finger
Watch it evaporate because I can never exist
Blurry vision with vivid hallucinations
Groping, touching, watching the fiends that are all there and
panic in a frenzy of orgy
We all live in a lonely plain addicted or not
Desolate drugged dreams with insanity as our host
Interactions are meaningless in the normal
reality of the sober world
Walking breathing Zombies trudging through 8-12 hour shifts
Seeking closure to the hatch they think
may have escaped from
Temporary disruption for the boring lives of
souls seeking a journey
Bite off more than you can chew then you become the victim
Ass bitten and with over indulgence and
become one of the others
The stage of life is where I am with a bass line bouncing me
into reality's mouth
Two stars on my shoulders that used to burn bright

What to do
Kiss your Life up against the wall of confusion
Or beg the World to stop watching me like a peeping tom
And let me conversate
What will I say I have no clue
I'm a loser through and true...

STABILITY OVERRIDE

Life of troubles
Life of sadness
Life of chaos
Life of loss
Not sending out an S.O.S.
I can do fine by myself
Too many emotions inside
Caring too much
Makes you care no more
Trying to find the way back
That person years ago
That road back is hard to travel
Cracks and pot holes
Lanes washed out
Makes me want to stop
Take another drink
A sip to the lips
A hit to the heart
A shot to the mind
A swallow to the soul
Now I am doing just grand
Deep in that well
Memories bring back so many
Many faces and times
People trying to stop my path
With respect in their hearts
To listen wasn't an option
Should have
Sinking is no longer shallow
Deeper you go
Suffocate in the misery
Gone at last
Or maybe so

TALENT BURIED IN JEALOUSY

Talent buried in jealousy
Broken words
Why does the beginning return to a dead end always
Suffer and cry but tears dropped are worthless
When the one you love fails to hear and understand
Pointless acknowledgements & various bullshit keep eyes wide
open
Covered in glossy alligator clear residue
Mr.What plays through my mind
Across the fucking universe
But in the end of all ends it's a fucking waste
Boy hits fucking car Good Lord
Eastern dreams coupled with Western promises although
good & 100%
Just mystical trickery in the Spirits that doubt...
I triple doubt...
My Soul is once again lost...

TELEVISION TRANSFERS THE SKY

My infection reduces your inebriated underrated rejection
Hate you possess and stress because a smile crosses my face
It is your fault alone
Even though your parents bore a wide body troll
I've inflicted nothing on you
But you wish to own my magic:

Happiness

Your violating views are nothing but a barbed wire stop sign of
hate
Fumigating with jealousy your soul is smaller than the most
sweetest tiny insect
Feeding off of others you suck the blood dry like a twilight
with no imagination
Inmates running the asylum with eyes glazed in frost
Strange days occur over rainbow filled pots of coal
Hundreds or thousands the many aren't well off good
33% doesn't change the soul
Evil still dwells with in you
Assassinate
Terminate
Brutally debate
Views won't change
Once wicked
Always vile

TEMPORARY DETENTION CENTER
MINUS THE PERKS

Eyes on the floor and don't move a muscle
Unless you want them spread apart for future enjoyment
Regret what you wish for but you would have never if you
weren't caught
Caught up in this web the spider wraps eight around you
Hard pointing appendages with venom on the
side if you try to flee
Weaving through your mind which was a neglected garden
Try to water the dying thoughts that wanted to bloom
Hands behind back with bondaged restraints
that once felt good
Bent over backwards with a little room to spare
Squirm as you might but the gag is in your mouth
Memory jogged with a runner sprinting around your head
Slept with their daughter, wife, husband, friend & secret lover
Interconnected with paths that lead to
a blissful elevated ambiance
Each one didn't know about the other due to excessive intake
Time rests for no one and they didn't have
an exemption to partake
Stupidity lies in the bloodshot eyes of the
beholder no matter how blind
Recounting the westward flee with hopes of escape
A statement of invalid facts with perfectly true lies
Welcome to your new world
Greet them with lies glowing in your eyes
They will dim so quickly
Then burn out

THE ART OF ADDICTION

Side to side eyes snake
What is watching me
Demons or Angels
Protecting or guiding volumes of confusion
Holding my hand as I tread the misery of life
Thrusting my head into the toilet of reality
Back and forth the song becomes routine
Shivering with the smell of fear
Stand and tremble or bow and indulge
Far above the ground excessive pleasure is what you seek
Towers of brightness with a twist of lime
Blizzard winds shooting all through you
Wide eyed at 4am just can't stop
The feeling blows through your mind and body
Pushing to the edge of stupidity
Bloodshot eyes or tears of pain
The lower levels of humanity revisited
Not the desire of the flesh that keeps you going
Numb adrenaline keeping you wired
For the moment live for that high
Yet death would be so much better
Her arms wrapped around me just don't let go
Hold on tight and pull me down
That last great orgasm
I'm looking forward to saying hi to my friends

THE BITCHINESS OF THAT
BEAUTIFUL GOD NAMED KARMA
(A personal Message to an Asshole)

I Love Karma she visits me often
So now to the problem:
Walking with the Gods or so you think
Above the law but you're just an idiot
Fuck with the meek and prove your paper certificate
intelligence
Care taker for the human race you'll never achieve
Blood sucking Napoleon complex you possess
Step off your step stool and look into Life
Fucked me once but you can't fuck me twice
I won't even classify you as bitch
You are so much lower than that
Stupidity of your so-called family values
I get fucked up the ass after the fact
Yet you are a pretend doctor and didn't advise your relative
Uh May I Say...
FUCK YOU!!! X 333
You failed but I get the blame with a filthy smirk
Results were fine no complications you fucking tool
A wooden one with splinters irritating all around you
Including your family oh poor them
It's her fault for breeding with you
Time evolves and I have a seizure
Did you give a holy fuck cause supposedly you are a faux God
Nope you didn't even know me other than fucking me royally
And that's an intimate thing not even a kiss
Now time moves on and you are in the same situation
Seizures galore and now you are so fucked
I laugh with glee and no sympathy

I'm the real thing unlike you
Don't fuck with a Fool who has a tainted soul that
can't be revived
Angels & Satan are creation of God
You are neither
I'm both and more than you can ever be
Like Caustic:
"I Won't Clip My Wings for Anyone"

THE CHALK MARKS THE SPOT

The chalk marks the spot
The last time you tumbled
Lost your sanity and pride
Unconscious and lost
For the last time but resurrected
Again and again to feel the pain
So mouth watering tasty
You feel the burn in the pit of your stomach
The warmth smolders within
Trying to destroy the damage of the past
A curb your pillow
The back seat of a car your bed
The doorstep of a neighbor your place to sleep
Rest for a moment then return to the binge
Draw a line on what is the last or next drink
Crossed it already it's so far behind
The winds of time already covered it with dust
Then Mother nature pissed on it soaking it wet
Just to make sure you'll never find your way back
Society to blame or so you wish
You are the fool drowning in it all
Misery loves company and you have twins
Dual demons of deceit that lick your eyeballs
Wetting them with an appetite for the drops of juice
The only atmospheric comfort to calm the soul
Two more sleeping pills then another shot
Sleeping beauty the goal
A content corpse the result

THE DAUGHTER OF PAIN & SUICIDE

Great
Fucked up again
Left in the gutter of life with stagnant water flowing by
The liquid of life stained with my blood that has decayed
Tainted with misery and self-hate beyond
anything you could imagine
Painful and wicked with the spice of death
Goodbye my love
Goodbye
Misleading misadventures with a western
influenced chaotic thought lost
Virgin ideas that go berserk at a moments notice with a pause
The seconds tick until the alarm rings with
sound-scape like a whirlpool
Twirling down into the undercurrent of life
where I dwell without a care
Inspired by the fuck of no God
Blessed by the Saints of disillusion
Cursed by the demons of appetite
Spider cloaked bracelets hang from your wrists
jingling with their pristine noise
Onyx earrings embedded into the abdomen
of spiders showcase your ears
Failure to bring you up from the depths of our
financially challenged life
The smile I once had is now petrified upside
down with no resolution
Everything I lived for
Everything I wanted
Everything my scattered mind dreamed of beyond
its limits is unjustified

The feather in the sky as the bird flies over
It drifts away floating down to its final place
I didn't float
I dropped like a Zeppelin on fire
With nothing worth saying
A scorching path to disturb the remains
Done for now even though you may regret our relationship
I did it all for you but addictions ruin more than 3 lives at a
time
Forgive me
Now I can't continue the cycle

THE FRAILITY OF DEATH AND DIRECTION

Hidden home of horrors
Bad spirits baring their teeth so pointed
Towards the direction of wisdom damaged
Company of the drugged
The evolution of man is a pack of hybrid lies
Dressings for the dead
Colors so bright they won't miss you if they take one last look
Questions beaten so badly the answers are nervous
Gag balled and ass fucked by your own devious ways
Tomorrow will never be a new day
Situation the same
Sober up, off the sauce, cold turkey
Ingested nothing of an ill path
Yet you are gone
Despoliation of your morals
Goblins kissing your toes
Licking them with glee as if dipped in sauce
Or your cum drenched fantasy of the previous night
The scent is what the wolves like to savor
The taste even more divine
Were will you go
Little fucked up Riding Hood
Frugality of the feelings
Even though buried below
They remember and ponder
Frenzied thoughts and wonder fly like an evil Angel
Spiraling down from her place so high
What was that kiss farewell for
Quick lock death
Perhaps God doesn't exist
So slaying the demons won't matter at all

Kiss, kiss bye-bye only fault
The direction of your shattered path
And what is being paid
The Addiction of life

THE SAD FLIGHT OF PROGRESS

Elevated above or so we think
Cable cars and subways running our veins deep inside
Long way from the bottom but you don't see
we are already there
Sid and Nancy a pair to remember but can't us too
Your charisma is playing tricks on me
The world stops when you fall in love
Time moves neither forward or back it just takes a break
Day seems like eternity
Kisses linger for ages
The smell of sex implanted in your nostrils
The beautiful odor giving you flash backs
of incredible orgasms
Moments of bliss and enthusiasm
I hate myself for dreaming of holding you
Because if I didn't dream I won't miss
The soft watermelon delights of your tiny perfect lips
The worst thing to be hooked upon for anyone is love
Usually it's the first thing that grabs hold and
fucks with our unbalanced system
After that frustrated and fucked we try to replace it
With another soul or another substance
Reaching for that high where the Angels sang
and we touched Heaven
Love is what causes all addictions
Without it we would be calm and plain
Normal and sane
Without hurt or tears that the demon loves to lick away
Love conquers all was the saying but open your eyes
Love only conquers because it destroys entirely like an atom
bomb inside your emotions
Blowing you away into bits and pieces never
remembering your precious core

THE SMALL SMELL OF VOMIT

Botox dreams
110 pound wish
Saliva drying on your face
Implants expecting to burst
Man is your enemy
Yet the idiots are those you wish to please
Gym is your savior
Diets your God
Skating on that frozen lake
The thin line between you and they
Keep pushing yourself
Scraping the ice til it cracks
Plunge into society
They welcome you with impaired views
Mary Poppins waiting at the chimney
Blowing smoke up your ass
Follow and fall
That's where you are headed
Her umbrella won't cover the lies
Your low self esteem
Your lack of self worth
The energy of erections
That do not care of your value
Coiled around the toilet
Porcelain the hidden friend
Empty yourself
Then do it all over again

THE TRIP OF-(NOT TO)-HEAVEN

The comet of your fear burns in your fingers
Your flame to heaven blazing with a glory
Toke the pipe
Down the bottle
Snort the excitement
Sins will always follow your path
Extend your hand and grasp them
Shattered dreams of light laid neutral
Melting conjunction of the past to present
Sanctuary perhaps beautiful in death
Angry songs of Angels shower down
Better by you to report your friend
To the demons within
I'm a fiend
And for my purpose
It's more than
Anything you could seriously imagine
Everyone knows
Fused with regret
Infested with love
Impaled with burnt contemplation
Beliefs deceased on a smoking field
Secrets crawling the attic of your mind
Furious with the need to escape
Thoughts best kept quiet
Sealed lies that can wake the dead
Dime store hoodlum dreams of grandeur
Faith in betrayal
Emptiness in honor

Loneliness in the reliance of self
The sky crying its tears of regret
Rain from Heaven I feel upon my face
Angels urine soaking down upon me
The only reward for the faith never known

THE WEAPONS OF VOICE

The weapons of voice
The lips of lies
I'm all your father warned you about
Your mother dreams of me
Spreads her legs for that next embrace
Maybe bringing her closer to that heaven she once knew
Only if he knew that attention misguided is the
downfall of all armies
Dictators and Liars
Fools and Kings
Jokers and Lovers
All fall for me
Pistachio cake dreams
Clovers and Clubs with Cupid at the side
Arrow in hand dipped with the venom of lust and lure
My extension into the soul is always doubted
but the grip is strong
The monster under the bed claws dripping
wet with your sweat
Licking its maw with your regret and prayers to
some invisible Gods
Fuel for the wicked and down
And I am as cruel as they come
The revolution is me turning the tricks before they are tricked
Disguises of the mind so fancy free accept what
I give and on you move
Gutter star dreams with inflections of the wet I
leave in your mouth
Exploding loins and desires I bury the cannon
deep in your being
Around the corner you know I am lurking

Wonderland delights but I'm right behind
you no need to hide
I'm there with you and every vice licking my
teeth for the taste

THE WORST CRIME IS...

Betrayal
When you crawl into bed at night
Hoping for beautiful dreams
Things are not all right
They never will be
You're so transparent
That in reality
You don't exist
To kill a human
Put a knife in their chest
The end is quick
To destroy them
Lie and ignore
The worst torture
Beyond any death
Run along with your smile
Live with your laugh
Charm is a poison
Used so freely
Let us hope
That an angel pays you a visit
And plants cyanide in your soul

THREESOME DREAMS PACKED IN A CYLINDER

Behind closed doors the fantasies unfold
Jockey for position the best place for a view
A touch too perfect will this be the last
Good bye Hello lips licking for that climax
Hills and valleys with curves in colors flowing so smooth
Snatch the moment seize the day for as long as you can
Those few hours seem like an eternity
Like a solar eclipse it's a rare opportunity
Sore feelings fly away when the flesh is ignited nerves on fire
Robot moves you're grinding on the floor
Pound the pleasure enjoy the wickedness
Float on orgasms that roll faster then waves in Maui
Moving all over the couch nothing left untouched
Off to the kitchen then to the bedroom on top of the hutch
Restraints on wrists just pushing the high to another level
Tremble and shake like a fiend on the
deathbed breathing heavy
Hair wet and body glistening with heart racing
like the Indy 500
Unlimited values with bliss and warmth coursing through
expanded veins
One moment inside then the another out of body experience
Doggy style love with cushions so perfectly soft
Hold on tight and ride for a journey that lasts longer than a
day and night
Squeeze out every last drop then lap it up like there is no
tomorrow
Love isn't the answer, question or statement at hand
All for one and one for all
Favors passed around for tension free joy

Exposed crevices let's all the splendor slide right in
Magnificent fornication of the mind blows out the night sky
The ultimate threesome you'll ever experience
You, the syringe and the drugs...

THUNDERBOLTS OF PINK

Sweet meat for the tongue
Succulent juice for the throat
Undefined pleasure to consume with unabashed envy
The center of eternity
The treasure of life
The holy grail of flesh
The warmth of the ecstasy
Dragonfly delights with sugar coated dreams
Collapsing time and space the Goddess stands
Seductive aura with beauty that progresses past the future
The desire within cannot be contained
Black lips and dripping candlesticks
Legs and platforms expanding the beauty
Curvatures from neck to ankles so smooth
Spine so wicked it makes you moan
Jaw lines crafted by the Angels
Mouth created for seduction and orgasm
Feet crafted with delicate sultry care
Fingernails painted to scratch and rake backs
She is the dream the fantasy unlocked
Grinds with precision every move a spectacular dance
Enchanting and wicked with energy to spare
Locked and loaded in your mind, heart and being
You can't escape you feel like you are in Heaven forever
Rolling on waves like the perfect island get away
Bodies so hot and wet you slip into the tide
Relations with a Deity so spectacular
Like a rainbow of lust that never ends
Bound by the darkness and engaging positions
to floor the mind
Delight so intense your grin almost touches your eyes

Deep inside the pleasure rolls and rolls
Touching every fiber with gratification granted from
something beyond this world
Heaven with a little wicked hint of hell to spice the senses
beyond imagination

TICKY TICKY TIME FOR THE WICKED

Amazing claims from the home of fame that's painted nice
Walls of glass continue to shatter out towards the silent
It's so shocking the field we play in
Free losers doing what needs to be done
Nothing of importance or committed casual relationships
Party and Play like it's the last day
Mover or shaker all you care about if they can sway
Soul has been taken in a box with wheels
spinning like luggage
Stumbling searches produce bitter answers
Audience of three stroking your thoughts
A dark room lit with fluorescent residue
The go-go is a no-no with a slice of lime
Salt your mental wounds
You still don't get it even if it's transcribed
A fading memory in the disorder of the mind
Advanced armament like a Nantucket suicide
The beat goes on and on
Even if no one listens
On the poles or the back seat it's Halloween
Let's call it a divine day in the morning
A.M. sex is like no other with guilt sprayed on the wall
Sticky and hard with a journey that started 11 hours ago
It's coming to an end in more ways than one

TINCTURE ME

What's in your hands
May I get a glimpse
Can we share
Just a little bit
I could do the only thing I was capable of
I left you alone
Wanted what you had
Desired what you sipped
Gazed at the concoction
Lusted for your mix
Knew where to hide
Disguise myself
You belong to me
So I thought
Here we go
Another round of trails on the loop
Pray for me
Or shall I pray for you
We cancel each other
False fears and hopes
Sing with the dead
Waiting for us
Spaces saved for you and me
The ground is open
It's mouth waiting to feed
Death, Destiny or Error
It's all the same
It's you and me
Good bye my love
Or is it
Hello

TOKE TO A REVIVAL OF GOSPEL
AND SUCH LUCK

50 grams on the table only 3 to be used
Glass counters the fountains of youth with an expiration date
Stoned, intoxicated and flying with colors vivid and surreal
Covering all corners of the universe and
communication is good
Dorothy around the corner waiting for Tina
to show up on time
The brick road now urine soaked and faded no longer bright
and happy with life
Every shadow with a monkey casts doubt
The River of Shit spews it's toxins
Just take another shower and wash the poison away
Veins sick with an itch, urge and lust that can't be
comprehended
Flight to flight usually non-stop
Black treasure box of memories locked up
so tight only the mind can see
Super hero for a few minutes as we tumble
but just a Fool in reality
Crawl through the bushes of life searching
for a paradise beach
Maybe find that chest of sunken treasure
Disengage from personal defeats & dreams of glory
A fecund imagination when sober, straight and clean
Washes away in the currents of dismay and disgust
All those missing people in your life
The one's you wish you met
With an open hand and a hug to pull you
out of the murky swamp
Validate the situation

Eyes pinned open with dilated pupils
Friends in shady places with inverted frowns
Limited outlooks from minds on skinny paths
Regret
Regret
Regret
Hiking the snow covered mountains til you
find the green pasture
Some times the other side of the fence is definitely beautiful

TOMMOROW WILL HOLD YOU HOSTAGE

Once you fall down from those skies with flights
that were so high
Spinning and twirling the ground waits with open jaws
Teeth gleaming brighter than all the monsters under your bed
Locked inside yourself with no key in sight
Screams trapped in your throat like change
in a vagrant's pocket
Negative path cramped with thorns of devastation
No sign of help or a chance to dial the medics
Somewhere to go although lost in your bed
Tossing and turning with pain radiating from deep within
The prize of the day would be a few hours
of sleep in a deep coma
Losers never win so rest comes in slices of time
like a rotten apple
Fewer than three minutes no chance for
REM and the Sandman
Hired killers running through your veins just a day ago
Searching to eliminate under the disguise of dazzling pleasure
Now their claws are dredging your insides in a slow creep
Fuel running low like a dragster at the end of
its eight-second run
The mattress of life swallowing you an inch at a time
Colors of the world to black, gray and white
Teeth chattering with jack hammer precision and force
Stomach screaming as if a wallaby were trying to burst out
Damp sheets hugging you wrapped up in a protective cocoon
No butterfly dreams to emerge just maggots of failure
Bright orange moon illuminates the midnight sky
Just one more time you wish to touch those rays of light

Clouds rumble in accompanied by sound of rabid werewolves
with handcuffs in claws
Saliva dripping from their mouth thick and full of misery
Fly high to the sky that's all you want
Your guardian Angel's wings were clipped
before you were born
As yesterday did
Tomorrow will hold you hostage

TWISTED DEVOTION

Moonlight smiles
Liquor bottle kisses
Pharmaceuticals to invigorate the soul
Just cause for loss that has passed
Step right through me
Not even a gate
Just a buoy for the soul
Something to tether onto
Let the waves lap at your conscience
Tide pulling you out
Lures to the bottom
Currents of dread push the envelope
Hatred of self
Loss of faith in anything with life
Muddy rivers of thoughts filled with debris
Swollen and bloated essence bounces
Confused to either sink or swim
Empty in the great bath of existence
Smells of sickness coming through the pores
Vendetta of violence upon your own feelings
Delicious anguish the only reason to float
In that high that isn't life
But mind altering beauty that lasts for only a moment
The crack in reality flowing through sinuses
The white cloud you sniff is just a sheet to cover your sorrow
Damp sadness your blanket made of tears

VILLIANS & FRIENDS

A ray of light splitting into several obscure paths
Population coughs with visions so blurred
Your Carnal Saint of Heavenly lies licks his lips
Stalker, Rocker, Legend in his own mind
Moving through the shadows but still a clumsy Ninja
Thoughts dominated by stupidity and lust
M-11 Cobray stuck in his mouth but it was a tease
Lips to metal idiot wanted to taste the barrel of a gun
Give him a dildo cracked and decrepit with no lubrication
Fuck him 5 ways to Sunday til the Moon appears
Coming back for more like a loved starved puppy with rabies
Jump back with shock & awe slapped across your face
Eyes roll back like a demon possessed with a hit of ecstasy
Feels so wonderful full of poppy seed bliss
Although the ground around is poisoned with
putrid sewer lies
Thick sludge in the mind bogging down
once perfect firing synapses
Golden Gates cables of man-made wonder
couldn't tow you out
Bottomless pit of lies he's right around the corner
Glaring with envy in what he wishes to own and ruin
Nightmare Man with foul black odor churning inside his soul
Live but not let others the only concern
Step back baby it is time to burn
Run like the Devil while skipping rope
It's the noose that will choke
No escape
No hope
Invitation to the lunacy a slight mistake
The alleyway of life is a miserable path
Walk away from it if you have a chance
Please

VULTURES SCREAM

Once you spit Legends Never Die
So true you are alive in my lost cranium
Like shrapnel scattered through our minds the pain still lurks
Glorious people leave way too early with so
much left to present
While others with nothing to offer but bubblegum
mockery of art breathe
Respecting nothing, thanking no one, betraying true creativity
Gravel that was never smoothed to fit the commercial
space of the followers
Voice so blatant that a kiss to the lips that produced
it invoked exquisite dreams
Hell and Heaven you represented to all with an
appreciation to music and style
A Goddess that the lights illuminated beyond your
eyes that were blind
Never played the fool or the almighty but your heart was there
Good lurks within even when you sing a
different song that explodes
Animals saved and rehabilitated you did what your heart could
Did as you pleased never bit off more than you could chew
The blueprint for all hard rocking vocalists you set it down
Embedded it in concrete and let them tread your path
A few have traveled in your path showing their strength
Trying to emulate but never giving credit where it's due
Another few whispered your inspiration
that was stamped on their mind
Yet you were inspired by true heroes like Karen S.
You knew so much before anyone glimpsed it
The true priestess of kindness with a perfect flare
Light up the skies of auditory enlightenment

A plant eater that was verified with a gleam in your eye
Chambers of your heart and mind pondered for so long
You left us too quickly
The woods your environment that settled your soul
What you created
What you whispered
What you sang
The Angels playing each and every song
I'm nothing and everything but I hear
Your music is so clear in my head
You'll never die in my mind

WASHES OVER ME

Washes over me
The disgust and trust
Armor of bed sheets
Comforter of steel
Let me lay still in movement and breathe
Connection to the fucked
Train wreck to Heaven
Limousine to Hell
Coordinates of the diseased
Engineers of horrific demise
All haunt me from the inside
Rip me wide open
An autopsy of faith
Sterilize the evil bacteria of my being
Siphon the virus of decaying mind
Slay the waste of thought
Taxidermy of the soul
Put me back together
Place me back on the fence
Which side should I jump towards
Neither choice a winning combination
Negative or positive
So I just fall
Whole in unity doesn't exist
Stitching up the exterior fails
The return to the spiral of downward passage
The door of dread always locked
Exposes what has always been broken
The soul that can never be mended
The essence of the corrupt

WATER FOUNTAIN SUREVEILENCE

Invisible non-mass carrying monsters lurking about
The honor of a simple mess to cause the reward
of ruined flesh
Psychologist of abstract dreams colors upon the
walls illumine under black light
Dreams spray-painted over and over with new
coats of desolation
Erratic lines shoot out everywhere but return to the
root of all...
Serious lack of enjoyment with effortless smiles pushes back
Like the persecutor of life simplistic fun is not permissible
Higher ground but bar codes and cell bars hold back
with a brutal resistance
Participants all around willing to help but only want
to share your treasure
Horde and bolt your stash but they'll get the residue with you
fiending for it back
Preachers in your mind seeking to be bombed with
psychedelic grenades
Still going to rise up no matter who gets you down
Magnified although not justified right of passage looms
around the corner
Directors of low cost dreams masturbation hand
open waiting for the funds
Deal done quick and your mind is racing for the next rapid fix
Once upon a time the security device in your
mind might have said no
Now broken and battered it doesn't operate worth a
good God damn
Scattered deliberation with philosophical schemes
tainted by remorse

Emotional strings severed and flying in the
typhoon ersatz air stream
Conversations full of worthless banter referring
back to your thesaurus of drugs
Dinosaur entries with every man made, home made,
earth made & mind made listed
Wonders of mind candy full of capacity arcing the
rainbow of joy
Gene mystery of icons who raised you on the TV and Radio
Beat down and skulking in the shadows of neon alleys
Escaping to the outside with the dregs in hand
Clutch it tight
Open your eyes wide
Kiss the night and hope it's not your last good bye
Gremlins of Greed waiting around the bend

WERE NOT...

No one is perfect
Yet we strive for perfection
And to be judged in their eyes as something beautiful
Life goes on...
Bare your soul with unflinching pride
Be proud of who you are and what you stand for
Or keep your secrets invisible well hidden inside
A carefully designed box you have crafted over the years
No matter who you meet in life
Each and every individual that crosses your path
If it lasts for one minute or 20 plus years
When they look or think of you
There will be one trait, quirk or flaw
Personality or physical
From the past or present
That they wish you were not...

WHAT IS DEEP INSIDE

Caves of lost loneliness
Nightlights that shine on nothing
Steering wheel that guides to a lost path
Hide and seek with the ghosts
Looking for a sanctuary that will never exist
Tumbling over and over down the hill for no reason
Sleeping dogs lie but have no judgment
Content with their life and what they do
Consume and sleep
Play for a bit then sleep again
We consume over and over again searching for enlightenment
Something to light up our minds with an explosion
Like a flare from a boat in distress
Come and save us we are so alone
Murky waters in the dark night represent our thoughts so
dark and black
Nervous energy bottled up in that glass container
with a cork plug
Floating in the universe of the ocean with lost content
Whoever finds it will never provide a rescue or answers
Lost 333 times
Others cannot save us
Others don't care
We are the beacon that leads us to our demise
The rest just laugh as we float on by
Dead and bloated our souls soak up all the drugs and alcohol
Bamboo stalks sway with the wind ever so slightly
For an eternity they stand the test of the time
You, Me and We fall over with toothpick strength
Born losers or self made idiots
Perhaps both
Down to the ground we fall with no style or grace
Dust in our mouths as we spit out obscenities

WHEN WILL ALL OF IT FINALLY START

Hallways of people passing by without a care of |
who or what you are
Pizza for brains with mouths that couldn't be shut
due to too much TV
Always one thing in common that binds the careless together
Nothing matters despite truth or lies
spoken with criminal intent
Fields of bright flowers speed on by every minute of our life
They speed by so fast we have no clue how slow and pathetic
we originally were
Magnificent Magnolias marinating with weak murder
of the soul and mind
Carrying pistols of hate through the bar to place
back to your head
Music so loud the summons is never heard for
you to turn around and hear reason
Bang pop drip vessels in your mind pour out your soul your
heart keeping a perfect beat
Nightmares that can fill a cargo plane open up
wide and smell the coffee of disaster
Seeking it out they need and want it like broken hearts
need a cast of love
Bathroom follies and recklessness plead a
case for just one more hit
Where is the room so we can take it to another
level just a tad higher
Contracts of blood, needles liquor and smoke
no need to sign the dotted line
Looking beaten, battered & bruised the cracked mirror of life
never smiles upon you

Raped by the law and used by the rich zilch substance doesn't
exist inside your spirit
Unless it's white, thin and ready to play laid out in front of you
Life has failed you and Mr. Bright won't return your calls
when you are lucid
Scars seen and not seen may never be healed and more will
almost certainly follow
Here by mistake always the claim but whose inaccurate
blunder was that
Bullets in the ass might make you think twice but then again
we'll never know
Chased down dark streets with sniper packing a rifle to blow
your mouth out
The long pipe releasing its contents into your head with a
detonation once again
Days later trembling with 3 days of no sleep
you search for an answer
The hidden treasure that may cure it all
An abstemiousness diet of delight is all we really seek
Ask yourself if you really want it
When will all of it finally start

WHEN THE IMPORTANT SPEAK

When the important speak
They know our addictions
They know our problems
They know our mistakes
We are stuck in the pathetic past
We never listen no matter how close they are
Dare to be real and let go of our insecurities
Imaginary Demons battle for our minds
The Monsters are always hunting us
With a primary addiction and trouble to dispatch
Roomy eyes with wicked expectations
Frames of lethal muscle built on foundations of granite
Abuse for the meek for their scarred hearts
deflect the hate inside
Constricted hearts still bleed madly
Concussions left on emotions still swollen and tender
Magic man in the alley with an antidote to remedy the purple
tinged blues
Drivel on puddles of faux tears mixed with invading chemicals
The price to be divine is your black soul locked in a decaying
box of disease

WITHOUT A NAME

On the frontline of your destruction
You murder me in 101 ways
Without a 21 gun salute
You bury my memory in the gutter
Hiss and spit at all who loved me
Fools, idiots and hookers in your eyes
Stab and ruin me again
Your mouth chews on my flesh
Tears of a reptile drip from you
The blood spreads onto the ground
Heavy dents with disturbed emotion
The March of pain down my spine
Doze off into the atmosphere
Let me glide away
Sharp shooter of deceit
Rifle laced bullets into my dreams
Rip the cord
But not a parachute
Casket of loving misery
Lid slammed shut
We have known each other for so long
The intimate times spent
You urinate on my flesh
Soak me in your deception
Drown me in treachery
Life jacket of dread
Bond of anonymity
Confused explosions
Alcohol
Love

YOUR STORY TO TELL
(CLARIFICATION)

Welcome loser
Hello fool
Greetings idiot
Good day junkie
Top "O" the morning clown
Inverted smile
Hello my not
Salutations winner
Tulips and daffodils
Burnt to a crisp
My soul is cindered
Your life moves on
Just a vessel of pain
A smuggler of pleasure
Skin covered lies
Burrow to the soul
Empty
Good bye...

LAST CORRESPONDENCE TO THE GODS

Their existence is a theory only a dead man can prove
The world grinds on an axis making all dizzy
with the wrong type of desire
Sea of madness so vast it has room to swallow all of the
population with space to spare
Assassinate the innocent with so called holy warriors
Devouring the meek in your machines of horrors
What will become of those that fade in the corner
Trying to hide from the evil inflicted
Creators, destroyers, annihilators, tricksters and
jokesters with a polished craft
Secrets of heaven with delicate locks now rusted solid
Elevators to paradise always closed and
under supposed construction
Isle of bewilderment open for business twenty-fours a day with
a revolving door
Conjuring up religions that ultimately equal the sum of 0+0
Nothing at the beginning, middle or finally the last few
moments of the final destination
A cemetery of dead prophecies but did any
of them survive and become fact
Your so-called light upon frozen dreams will never melt them
free from iceberg coffins
Mystical mirages with a treasure chest of
wisp smoldering visions
Unconvincing with all the chaos in life new
designs have been erected
Keep it clandestine but recruit the bamboozled with such ease
Natural disasters with more acts to follow wiping out millions
Charismatic effigies won't save the babies and
children that are already dead

Written words of illusion save no one from wars
invoked in your names
Conflicts settled with violence floats in the air everyday with
your smiles shining down
Yet your legions remain strong with judgmental minds
Shackled and chained they are slaves to all of your lies of
fabricated truth
Submission to a higher power a pathetic way to preach fiction
that they believe
Hearts trapped in a dungeon of a fairy tale gone wrong
Lethal apples waiting to be bitten line the streets from point A
to B and all in-between
Hanging from the trees that provide cover in a
lighter shade of darkness
Against the wind millions feel your love filled wrath
Falling on their knees begging for mercy wishing and looking
for a miracle
Cross hairs of the gun your only true sign with
a knife in the chest
Hands unseen squeezing hearts until they are
withered and empty
Circle around the cross is the enchantment used
to target the honest and true
Hooligan icons spread out through the world for worship
Entombed in your religions that fail at every broken turn
You pour into their minds like a raging river then
drown them at the dam
Chance of enlightenment swimming down river free to lure
more untarnished souls
Hollow promises of seeing the light through the darkest days
Although the bulb has been burned out for
eternity and a night
Blind, deaf and always mute as an empty library whose walls
could tell many tales

Crowds you beckon erupt into verbal executions for non-
believers who fail to accept
Petitioning for signatures from any witless clown
with prayers to follow
Turn theirs back then everything including your false
promises disappears like magic ink
Their minds scattered like ashes in turbulent winds of a
hurricane that will never die
Trying to wipe their slate clean with a sponge made of rock
and sand for acts committed
Your righteous words are more like rash orders that itch the
skin with disturbance
Masks constructed from your outrageous imaginations to
deceive and entice
Sending Angels who are really hypnotic
devils with sin to spare
I should know I have three that always surround me
Their names are Bad, Terrible and Worse
Tormenting me with their trickery and
deceit at the highest level
The entourage of deviant mischievous sprites
always stay a whisper away
No heavy sleep until you are clinically dead
I'm way past that in a deep slumber like the beauty that sleeps
Only with hints of grotesque for nothing beautiful
resides in a lifeless husk
If there is good in the world I have yet to witness it with
bloodshot eyes
Questions I hurdle plummet back down after
bouncing against the dense skies
Landing in the mountains of my mistakes buried for eternity
never to be answered

The disease I have will never cease and none
of you will make it vanish
Can't make it disappear like a fool blindfolded walking
through a minefield at 3A.M.
Addiction was enrapturing now it's the demon of burden
Hand reached out many times only to be slapped away with
laughter in the background
Chasm of despair continued to sink even deeper until it
became bottomless
Fouled and weathered friends obstruct my thoughts with their
clouds of confusion
The same way you obscure the devout and misplaced
My fury surges like white water rapids bouncing
against the boulders of life
Directions of escape clearly the path that must be taken
Maybe I have found it as I hold my breath with nerves
dead as petrified wood
I know your games and what exactly all of you are up to
The worst has already happened in the minds
of people around me
Their tongues are wrong for it is yet to come
I'll be arriving to visit with a mind that's numb, anger to burn
and so not willing to conform
Now is the time to test that theory
The Beginning of the end...

ABOUT THE AUTHOR

———❧❧❦❧❧———

(17 FACTS/FICTION THAT AREN'T LIFE OR
DEATH ABOUT HIM):

1. FOOL

2. SPACE CADET(or KADET as he likes it)

3. IDIOT (all men are so deal with it)

4. DAY DREAMER

5. LOST NUT

6. NOT SO CLEAR DIMLY BRIGHT INNOVATIVE
THOUGHTS

7. MEMORY DEFICIENT

8. NINJA

9. LAID BACK

10. OPEN MINDED

11. DODO HEAD

12. NEEDS AN ENEMA (alien probes remember)

13. ANGEL (well ok, to a very few)

14. SHOE ADDICT

15. HAPPY

16. TIME TRAVELLER (micronauts rock)

17. MONKEY BOY

Find him lurking at these various loci:

Vampirefreaks.com/miguelbizarre
Goodreads.com/miguelbizarre
FaceBook:
Miguel Bizarre
myspace.com/miguelbizarre
email:
miguel@miguelbizarre.com
twitter:
@miguelbizarre

THANK YOU FOR ENDURING!!!